C   IN

STUDIES ON THE CONSTITUTIONS

OF THE

SOCIETY OF JESUS

This book is Number 1 in

Series IV: Study Aids on Jesuit Topics

IGNACIO IPARRAGUIRRE, S.J.

CONTEMPORARY TRENDS
IN
STUDIES ON THE CONSTITUTIONS
OF THE
SOCIETY OF JESUS

ANNOTATED BIBLIOGRAPHICAL ORIENTATIONS

Translated by

DANIEL F. X. MEENAN, S.J.

THE INSTITUTE OF JESUIT SOURCES

St. Louis, 1974

This book is an authorized translation, with adaptations, of *Constituciones de la Compañia de Jesús: Orientaciones biblio-gráficas*, by Ignacio Iparraguirre, S.J., published in 1973 by Centrum Ignatianum Spiritualitatis, C.P. 9084, 00100 Roma, Italy.

IMPRIMI POTEST: Very Reverend Leo F. Weber, S.J.
                   Provincial of the Missiouri Province
                   March 9, 1974

IMPRIMATUR: Most Reverend Charles R. Koester
                   Vicar General of St. Louis
                   March 13, 1974

© 1974   The Institute of Jesuit Sources
          Fusz Memorial, St. Louis University
          3700 West Pine Blvd.
          St. Louis, Missouri 63108

Published through the aid of funds
donated by the late Mr. James L. Monaghan
of Milwaukee, Wisconsin,
1867- 1963,
in memory of his brother,
Reverend Edward V. Monaghan, S.J.,
1879- 1922,

CONTENTS

ON SERIES IV: STUDY AIDS ON JESUIT TOPICS

Father Ignacio Iparraguirre, S.J., long a member of the Institutum Historicum Societatis Iesu in Rome, ranks among the foremost Ignatian scholars of our century. His unexpected death on October 6, 1973, is a great loss to studies on Jesuit spirituality and a cause of sorrow to his friends. One of his last works was a little volume aimed to be helpful during the preparation of General Congregation XXXII of the Society of Jesus, *Constituciones de la Compañía de Jesús: Orientaciones bibliográficas,* published by the Centrum Ignatianum Spiritualitatis, which is housed in the Jesuit Curia in Rome. Father Daniel F. X. Meenan, S.J., Assistant Director of that Centrum, translated Father Iparraguirre's volume into English; and the Institute of Jesuit Sources is privileged and happy to present his version in this present book, *Contemporary Trends in Studies on the Constitutions of the Society of Jesus: Annotated Bibliographical Orientations.* Both the translator and the undersigned editor have made adaptations, chiefly additions, which adjust the book a little more closely to the needs of English-speaking readers.

With this present little book, too, the Institute of Jesuit Sources is inaugurating a new series of publications: Series IV: Study Aids on Jesuit Topics. This is an addition to the three previous series: I, Jesuit Primary Sources, in English translations; II, Modern Scholarly Studies about the Jesuits, in English translations; and III, Original Studies, composed in English. The New Series IV is an effort toward solving the following problem.

From its inception the Institute of Jesuit Sources has been oriented toward the publishing of scholarly books of quality.

Such books, carefully selected, obviously have advantages, especially the long-lasting values arising from their presence
in libraries. But this orientation, if maintained exclusively,
also entails two disadvantages which are especially hampering
and costly in our present era of rapid developments and changes:
the lengthy time required for the writing and editing, and the
expense of typesetting, printing, and binding with cloth.

There is another class of writings, such as doctoral dis-
sertations, study aids, bibliographies, monographs, preliminary
editions, and documented or well founded reflections, which
have a different but genuine value. These are, in many cases,
not yet the finished, polished, and fully matured scholarship
ordinarily found in the volumes published by university presses.
But they are a step toward such scholarship. They contain much
sound material which is truly helpful to interested persons and
which would remain unavailable if postponed until high perfection could be attained. In many cases such delay could all too
easily turn out to be an instance in which the dreamed of best,
which may never come, is the enemy which defeats the presently
attainable good.

This new Series IV will consist of studies in this category.
Hopefully, too, it will offer some solution of the problem sketched
above. An effort will be made to keep the books or booklets in-
expensive, through the use of typewriter composition and paper-
back bindings. Editorial time and cost, too, will be kept as
low as possible, with the responsibility for details being al-
lowed to rest more fully on the authors than on the editors of
the Institute of Jesuit Sources.

In the designing of this new series, many helpful ideas
have been taken from the somewhat similar procedure in scholarly
publishing which has been launched by the Council on the Study
of Religion, for example, in the two "Dissertation Series" re-
spectively of the American Academy of Religion and of the Society of Biblical Literature. The rationale of these series is
well described by Robert W. Funk and Robert A. Spivey in the
Bulletin for the Council on the Study of Religion, Volume IV,

number 3 (June, 1973), pages 3-13, 28-29, and 36-37; and also, at greater length, in the *Report of the Task Force on Scholarly Communication and Publication*, edited by George W. MacRae, S.J. (1972, available from the Council on the Study of Religion Executive Office, Waterloo Lutheran University, Waterloo, Ontario, Canada). Indebtedness to this helpful information and example is gratefully acknowledged.

George E. Ganss, S.J.
Director, the Institute of Jesuit Sources
The Institute of Jesuit Sources

BIOGRAPHICAL SKETCH

IGNACIO IPARRAGUIRRE, S.J., (1911-1973)

To attempt here a biography which would do justice to the
personality, zeal, competence, and charitable helpfulness of
Father Ignacio Iparraguirre is impossible. But it is appropriate to give at least some indication of the life and achieve-
ments of this priestly person to whom those interested in studies
on Ignatian and Jesuit spirituality owe so much.

Ignacio Iparraguirre was born in Bilbao, Spain, August 30,
1911. He entered the Society of Jesus on August 31, 1926, at
Loyola, Spain, where he made his novitiate and juniorate. Then,
with Spain ravaged by civil war, he made his philosophical studies at Marneffe, Belgium, his regency at Tournai, his theology
at Valkenburg, Holland, and (1939-1940) at Durango and finally
Oña, Spain (where he was ordained a priest). He went through
his tertianship under the well-known Antonio Arregui at Manresa.
Then in 1941 he was sent to Rome to prepare himself for his Ignatian studies in the Historical Institute of the Society of
Jesus. After his reception of a doctorate in Church History
from the Gregorian University in 1946, he lived at that Historical Institute until his unfortunate and unexpected death on
October 6, 1973, possibly through an accidental fall, possibly
through a heart attack which caused the fall.

His life at Rome was one of zealous dedication to the field
of Ignatian scholarship. Yet he found time to accompany his re-
search and writing with continual pastoral ministries; and he
spent considerable time and effort in conducting the Spiritual
Exercises. From the extensive bibliography of his books and
articles we cull the following highlights.

I. On St. Ignatius

Espíritu de san Ignacio de Loyola: Perspectivas y actitudes ignacianas de espiritualidad. Bilbao, 1958. Pp. 207.

Repertoire de spiritualité ignatienne (1556-1615). Subsidia ad historiam Societatis Iesu, no. 4. Rome, 1961. Pp. xx + 268.

Obras completas de san Ignacio de Loyola. Edición manual. Transcripción [de textos], introducciones, y notas de Ignacio Iparraguirre, S.J., con la Autobiografía . . . por C. de Dalmases, S.J. 2nd. edition, revised. Biblioteca de autores cristianos, no. 86. Madrid, 1963. Pp. xvi + 1,021.

Orientaciones bibliográficas sobre san Ignacio de Loyola. 2nd edition, revised. Subsidia ad historiam Societatis Iesu, no. 1. Rome, 1965. Pp. xvi + 200.

II. On the Spiritual Exercises

Historia de la práctica de los Ejercicios espirituales de san Ignacio de Loyola.

Vol. I: *Práctica de los ejercicios de san Ignacio en vida de su autor (1522-1556).* Rome, 1946. Pp. 54* + 320.

Vol. II: *. . . hasta la promulgación del Directorio oficial (1556-1599).* Rome, 1955. Pp. 48* + 588.

Vol. III: *Evolución en Europe durante el siglo XVII.* Rome, 1973. Pp. 32* + 587.

The above volumes are nos. 3, 7, and 36 of Bibliotheca Instituti Historici Societatis Iesu.

Directoria Exercitiorum Spiritualium (1540-1599). Ed. I. Iparraguirre, S.J. No. 76 of Monumenta Historica Societatis Iesu. Rome, 1955. Pp. xii + 869.

Ejercicios Espirituales: Commentario pastoral por Luis González,
S.J. y Ignacio Iparraguirre, S.J. Biblioteca de autores
cristianos. Madrid, 1965. (Pp. 129-346, "Tendencias y
orientaciones de los interpretes principales," are by
Father Iparraguirre.)

*Vocabulario de Ejercicios Espirituales: Ensayo de hermenéutica
ignaciana.* Rome: Centrum Ignatianum Spiritualitatis, 1972.
Pp. viii + 216.

George E. Ganss, S.J.

In this time of preparation for the coming General Congregation XXXII, there is a genuine need for an adequate knowledge of the present state of various studies about the chief matters of our Institute, and particularly about the Constitutions.

Our present concern for return to our sources, for authenticity, and for renewal necessarily depends on an analysis of the essential elements related to our various structures. Only through such study can we know which elements ought to be retained as essential and which to be subjected, to a greater extent, to adaptation.

It is for this reason that I thought it useful to make available my work, *Constituciones de la Compañía de Jesús: orientaciones bibliográficas*. This booklet, No. 1 in the series "Subsidia" published by the Centrum Ignatianum Spiritualitatis at the Jesuit Curia in Rome, presents very succinctly the results obtained from the labors of specialists on themes relating to St. Ignatius' Constitutions.

Jesuits today, of course, are much occupied, and even over-occupied, with other matters. Moreover, many of these studies are scattered in various periodicals and written in languages not known to all. Father Daniel F. X. Meenan, S.J., a member of that Centrum Ignatianum, has now translated and slightly adapted my Spanish text into this present English work, published by the Institute of Jesuit Sources in St. Louis. Consequently, English-speaking readers will now have at hand within a few pages the substance of these more lengthy investigations.

I have limited myself to setting forth the core ideas of the various works. But there are some who will desire to go into various aspects in greater detail. Therefore I have also given exact bibliographical data. For those who want merely some knowledge of the present state of investigation, the mere reading of these summaries will be sufficient. But all will find here guides to material for further study according to their own desires.

For still other aspects relating to St. Ignatius, my earlier study remains useful: *Orientaciones bibliográficas sobre san Ignacio de Loyola* (Rome: Institutum Historicum Societatis Iesu, 1965). Citations from that work in the present one are indicated by the word *OrientBibliograf*, and may serve as an introduction to the fundamental works on the life and spirituality of St. Ignatius.

Ignacio Iparraguirre, S.J.
Rome, June 10, 1973

CONTEMPORARY TRENDS

IN

STUDIES ON THE CONSTITUTIONS

OF THE

SOCIETY OF JESUS

A B B R E V I A T I O N S

Cons—*The Constitutions of the Society of Jesus,* in any edition
ConsMHSJ—*Sancti Ignatii de Loyola Constitutiones Societatis Iesu,* 4 volumes in the series MHSJ. For details see no. 4 below.
MHSJ—Monumenta Historica Societatis Jesu, the Historical Records or Sources of the Society of Jesus, in critically edited texts.
MonNad—*Epistolae P. Hieronymi Nadal,* 6 volumes in the series MHSJ.
OrientBibliograf—*Orientaciones bibliográficas sobre san Ignacio de Loyola,* by I. Iparraguirre, S.J. 2nd ed. rev. Rome, 1965.
RAM—*Revue d'ascétique et de mystique*
RazFe—*Razon y Fe*

PART I. EDITIONS AND TRANSLATIONS

A. *Bibliography*

1. *Dossier "Constitutiones"* A. Rome: Centrum Ignatianum Spiritu-
     alitatis, 1972. Pp. 327. In this paperback volume:
          Documentum I, pp. 5-20, is a bibliography on the Con-
     stitutions for the years 1956-1971, prepared by Emilio
     Anel, S.J.
          Documentum III, on pages 285-295, "Études et travaux
     sur les Constitutions de la Compagnie de Jésus, 1960-1971,"
     by Gervais Dumeige, S.J., surveys the past and present
     trends in the use and study of the Constitutions. It also
     gives an evaluation of many of the works listed just above
     in Documentum I.

2. *Archivum Historicum Societatis Iesu* (hereafter abbreviated *AHSJ*)
     33 (1964), 90-101, contains a bibliography by L. Polgar,
     S.J., of older works on the Institute, including works on
     the Constitutions.

3. Ignacio Iparraguirre, S.J, *Orientaciones bibliográficas sobre
     san Ignacio de Loyola*, Subsidia ad historiam Societatis
     Iesu, no. 1 (Rome: Institutum Historicum Societatis Iesu,
     2nd, ed., rev., 1965), remains a very helpful tool. Al-
     though the present annotated bibliography, *Contemporary
     trends in Studies on the Constitutions of the Society*,
     supplements and updates the section on the Constitutions
     (nos. 482-508, pp. 126-132), the original book of 1965
     contains much information which it was not found expedient
     to repeat in this present work.

4. Also, an extensive bibliography on the Constitutions, includ-
     ing a list of all the ninety-eight volumes published up
     to 1970 in the series Monumenta Historica Societatis Iesu,
     (hereafter abbreviated MHSJ) is available on pp. 358-370

of the English translation of the Constitutions by George
E. Ganss, S.J. (on which see no. 11 below).

B. *Editions*

1. *The Constitutions*

5. *Sancti Ignatii de Loyola Constitutiones Societatis Iesu.* MHSJ,
   Monumenta Ignatiana, series 3. 4 vols., (abbreviated hereafter as *Cons*MHSJ, I, II, III, IV). Rome: Institutum Historicum Societatis Iesu, 1934-1948).

   *Cons*MHSJ, I, *Monumenta Constitutionum praevia*, contains primary sources, documents, and papal bulls and
   briefs previous to 1556.

   *Cons*MHSJ, II, *Textus hispanus*, contains the four chief
   Spanish texts: the first, *a*, of 1549-1550, the second, A,
   written before the end of September, 1550; the third, B,
   also called the "autograph," of 1551-1552 but with correc-
   tions added until 1556; the fourth, D, a more critically
   edited Spanish text approved by General Congregation V in
   1594 and published in 1606.

   *Cons*MHSJ, III, *Textus latinus*, contains the critical
   text of the Latin translation which was approved, along
   with the Spanish original, by General Congregation I in
   1558. The Latin text was then published in printed form
   and appeared in 1558-1559.

   *Cons*MHSJ, IV, *Regulae Societatis Iesu (1540-1556)*,
   on which see no. 7 below.

6. *Obras completas de san Ignacio de Loyola. Edición manual.*
   Transcripción, introducciones, y notas de I. Iparraguirre,
   S.I., con la *Autobiografía de san Ignacio*, editada y ano-
   tada por Candido de Dalmases, S.I. Biblioteca de autores
   cristianos, no. 86. Madrid: La Editorial Catolica, 1952.
   2nd edition, revised, 1963.

   Pages 415-596 of this work contain a handy, scholarly
   edition of the Spanish text of the Constitutions, with

modernized spelling and helpful footnotes, by I. Iparraguirre, S.J.

2. *The Rules*

7. *Regulae Societatis Iesu (1540-1556)*. Edited by Dionisio Fernández Zapico. Rome, 1948. This is *Cons*MHSJ, IV, on
   which see no. 5 above.

   With the exception of one group, the Rules of Simão
   Rodrigues on pages 17-134, all these rules come from St.
   Ignatius or his collaborators in Rome.

C. *Translations*

8. German: "Die Satzungen der Gesellschaft Jesu aus den spanischen
   ubersetzt und eingeleitet von Mario Schoenenberger und Robert
   Stadler, S.J." Pp. 267-350 in *Die Grossen Ordenoregeln*.
   Menschen der Kirche, no. 8. Einsiedeln: Benziger, 1948;
   2nd ed. rev., 1961, pp. 323-411.

   The above contains only selections. A new German
   translation of the entire Constitutions by Peter Knauer,
   S.J., has been completed but not yet published.

9. French: Saint Ignace. *Constitutions de la Compagnie de Jésus*.
   Vol. I: *Traduction du texte officiel, notes et index par*
   François Courel, S.J. Vol. II: *Introduction à une lecture,*
   par François Roustang, S.J. *Traduction du texte primitif*
   par François Courel, S.J. La collection Christus, nos.
   23, 24. Paris: Desclée de Brouwer, 1967. Pp. 316 and
   292.

   For all practical purposes, this translation supplants the earlier version, *Les Constitutions des jésuites*
   avec les déclarations (France, 1762), 3 vols. A new edition and translation appeared in Paris in 1843. For the
   special circumstances which gave rise to this earlier version, see Sommervogel, *Bibliothèque de la Compagnie de*

Jésus, V, columns 79-80.

10. About the introductions of Roustang to the French translation of the Constitutions, and especially about his interpretation to the effect that Polanco's influence changed a more charismatic and spiritual mentality or coloring found in earlier texts into one more juridical, see: Michel Rondet, S.J., in *Christus,* 14 (1967), 259-268; Jesús M. Granero, S.J., in *Manresa,* 39 (1967), 235-244; Candido de Dalmases, S.J., in *AHSJ,* 43 (1967), 300-306; J. C. Guy, S.J., in *RAM,* 43 (1967), 353-356; Victor Codina, S.J., in *Selecciones de libros,* 4 (1967), 492-493; and Antonio de Aldama, S.J., in *Dossier Constitutiones A* (1972, and 1 above), pp. 29-95 and 121-129 (as indicated also in no. 16 below).

11. English: St. Ignatius of Loyola. *The Constitutions of the So-ciety of Jesus. Translated, with an Introduction and a Commentary,* by George E. Ganss, S.J. St. Louis: The Institute of Jesuit Sources, 1970. Pp xii + 420. 2nd printing, 1971.

This first English translation of the entire corpus of St. Ignatius' Constitutions, made from the Spanish and including the Formula of the Institute, presents them as a classic of spiritual doctrine and of the law of religious institutes. The Introduction presents Ignatius' spiritual world view, formed by his mystical religious experiences, to which he gave legislative expression in his Constitutions. This world view led him to his intense desire to be intimately associated with Christ in achieving God's plan of creation and redemption. The Commentary aims chiefly to bring out what Ignatius' terms and phrases meant to his sixteenth-century contemporaries and to give leads for further study. For reviews, see: A. de Aldama, S.J., in *AHSJ,* 40 (1971), 188-190; W. V. Bangert, S.J., in *Thought* 45, (1972), 475-476; F. Courel, S.J., in *RAM,* 46, (1970), 467-468; J. G. Dwyer, in *The Catholic His-torical Review,* 68 (1973), 640-641; D. L. Fleming, S.J., in *Review for Religious*, 30 (1971), 151; J. M. Granero, S.J., in *Manresa*, 43 (1971), 92-93; P. De Letter, S.J., in *The Clergy Monthly*, 35 (1971), 90; J. Lopez-Gay, S.J., in *Gregorianum*, 52 (1971), 198-199; Sister Caritas McCarthy, SHCJ, *The Way, Supplement 14* (1971), 33-45; L. Renard, S.J., in *Nouvelle Revue Théologique*, 95 (1973), 1022-1023; Sister M. Roman, O.C.D., *Spiritual Life*, 17 (1971), 159-160; A. Wilder, O.P. in *Cross and Crown*, 23 (1971), 100-102. Sisters Caritas McCarthy and M. Roman treat of the use of St. Ignatius Constitutions' by institutes of religious women.

This translation too, like the French, can be said to supplant a very scarce and little known earlier translation of the Constitutions (without the Examen and the Declarations), made from the Latin text of 1558 by a hostile non-Catholic and published in London in 1838, with a title page worded: *The Constitutions of the Society of Jesus. . . . Rendered into English from the Latin: with an Appendix, containing the Three Bulls for the Institution* [i.e., *Regimini*], *Suppression, and Restoration of the Order of Jesuits: and an Outline of the Present Condition of the Romish Church in this Kingdom. Caecum Scelus Omne.* The Introduction, notes, and appendix are strongly anti-Romish and anti-Jesuit, but the translations are accurate.

12. Polish. Ignacy Loyola: *Pisma Wybrane Komentarze.* Krakow, Wydawnictwo Apostolstwa Modlitwy, 1968. Vol. I, pp. 391-464. Translated by M. Bednarz, S.J.

This is a much abbreviated translation of the chief paragraphs with a summary of the contents of all the Constitutions.

13. Italian. Ignazio di Loyola, Sant'. *Costituzioni della Compagnia di Gesù. Traduzione del testo ufficiale spagnolo, note e indici e cura di Giuseppe Silvano, S.J.* Milano: Editrice Ancora, 1969.

This translation contains an Introduction by Ignacio Iparraguirre, S.J., who states that he was aided on some points by Maurizio Costa, S.J.

14. *Excerpta Constitutionum S. I.* Rome: Curia Praep. Gen. S.I., 1968.

This new set of selections was issued by Father General Pedro Arrupe on January 2, 1968, in accordance with decrees 20, nos. 1, 2 and also 19, nos. 14, 15 of General Congregation XXXI. These selections, differently from those in the well known *Summary of the Constitutions* of 1950, retain the sequence they have in St. Ignatius' original text, and thus they can be more readily and accurately interpreted according to their context and position in the Constitutions taken as a whole. They have been translated into the principal languages.

15. *Index de l' Examen Général et des Constitutions.* Paris: Christus, 1962.

This is a mimeographed brochure of 62 pages which lists in alphabetical order every Spanish word in the Constitutions and all of its occurrences. It was reprinted by the Centrum Ignatianum Spiritualitatis, Rome, in 1973 as no. 2 in its series of Subsidia.

D. *Sources and Composition of the Constitutions*

16. Arturo Codina, in his prologue to the critical edition of the Constitutions (*Cons*MHSJ, II, vi-cclx), explained the status in 1934 of studies about the sources and genesis of the Constitutions.

Dionisio Fernández Zapico did the same in 1948 in regard to the Rules, in the prologue of *Cons*MHSJ, IV, 2*-35*.

Since then important developments have occurred: (1) the codex was discovered on which Polanco was annotating the texts which he had copied from earlier orders as a preparatory work for the Constitutions (Aloysius Hsu, S.J., has published this in a lithographed edition as an appendix to his dissertation, *Dominican Presence in the Constitutions of the Society of Jesus* [Rome: Gregorian University, 1971]); and (2) various studies on the style of Polanco, above all that of Roustang in his *Introduction à une lecture* . . . (on which see above, nos. 9, 10).

These developments necessitated a reexamination of the entire problem from new points of view and on new bases, as can be seen from the reviews of Roustang's work, indicated above in nos. 9, 10. Antonio M. de Aldama, S.J., has made a detailed study of the various manuscripts and the various subsequent printed texts of the Constitutions, in his "La composición de las Constituciones de la Compañía de Jesús: Notas para la historia . . . ," in *Dossier "Constitutiones" A*, pp. 29-95, and his "Evolución de la Sexta Parte de las Constituciones en cuadro sinoptico," ibid., pp. 121-129. Roustang's studies, published in 1967, were based almost entirely on the printed texts found in MHSJ, especially *Cons*MHSJ, I and II (see "Introduction a une lecture," 9 above, especially p. 37). These later studies, based largely on scrutiny of the manuscripts in the archives of the Society in Rome, seem to show that many of Roustang's main contentions were made with insufficient evidence.

17. Additional works worthy of consultation are these:

Paul de Chastonay, S.J., *Die Satzungen* . . . , pp. 11-80, or *Les Constitutions* . . . , pp. 9-71 (no. 29 below).

Arturo Codina, S.J., "Regulae antiquorum ordinum et praeparatio Constitutionum S.I.," *AHSJ*, 1 (19732), 41-72.

Pedro de Leturia, S.J., "De 'Constitutionibus collegiorum' P. Ioannis A. de Polanco ac de earum influxu in Constitutionibus S. I.," *AHSJ*, 7 (1938), 1-30 and *Estudios Ignacianos* (no. 103 below), I, 355-387.

Hugo Rahner, S.J., "Ignatius von Loyola und die

aszetische Tradition der Kirchenväter," *ZAM*, 17 (1942), 61-77; also, translated into English as "Ignatius and the Ascetic Tradition of the Fathers," in *Ignatius the Theologian* (New York: Herder and Herder, 1968), pp. 32-52.

PART II. GENERAL COMMENTARIES

A. *In the Society before the Suppression*

18. Nadal, Hieronymus, S.J. *Scholia in Constitutiones et Declarationes S. P. Ignatii.* Prato, Italy, 1883. Pp. x + 435.

> The principal value of this work rests on the prestige or authority which arises from the author's proximity to Ignatius. He seems to have composed these scholia so as to comply with decree 51 of General Congregation I. General Congregation II examined them but did not confer any authority on them. They could serve "merely as directive, without any obligation" (*pro directione tantum, sine ulla obligatione*). In this work Nadal merely explains some particular points, for the most part very briefly.

> Many other comparable observations can be found in his "Exhortationes" in MHSJ, *MonNad*, IV, in which he explains various points of the Constitutions, and especially in his documents on the Institute which have been published in *MonNad*, V, *Commentarii de Instituto Societatis Iesu*, edited by M. Nicolau, S.J. (1962).

19. S. Petri Canisii. *Exhortationes domesticae, collectae et dispositae a Georgio Schlosser, S.J.* Ruremonde: Romen, 1876. Pp. iv + 475.

> Simple conferences, important for the personality of the author who was formed by Ignatius himself.

20. Manaraeus, Oliverius, S.J. *Exhortationes super Instituto et regulis Societatis Iesu, quas ante trecentos amplios annos provinciis Germaniae et Belgii tradidit.* Edited by Bruno Losschaert, S.J. Ruremonde: J. De Meester, 1912. Pp. 15 + 794.

> Some important data about Ignatius are found here and also about the primitive practice of some early customs.

21. Baltasar Alvarez, S.J. *Pláticas y exposición de las reglas*

generales de la Compañia de Jesús. Madrid: Razon y fe, 1910. Pp. 257. Also,

——— *Escritos espirituales. Introducción biográfica y edición* por Camilo M. Abad, S.J. y Faustino Boado, S.J. Barcelona: Flors, 1961. Espirituales espanoles, vol. 4. Pp. 516-706.

These conferences offer a commentary on the Summary of the Constitutions and Rules which Laynez published in 1560. They are conferences full of spiritual doctrine and unction.

22. Gil González Dávila, S.J. *Pláticas sobre las reglas de la Compañia de Jesús. Prólogo y edición de* Camilo M. Abad, S.J. Pp. viii + 833.

These are conferences given between 1585 and 1588 when González Dávila was provincial of Andalusia. He comments on the text of the Summary of the Constitutions and on the Common Rules, printed in 1580. In part he rises to the heights of spiritual principles and describes the spirit of the Society along its more general lines, and in part he descends to practice, and sets before our eyes "the road we must travel in order to arrive at the proper end of our vocation." The matter is set forth in a correct style, and he dialogues much of the time with "interlocutors." Alfonso Rodríguez made use of some portions of these conferences in his *Practice of Christian Perfection* published in 1609 (see Alejo Barjavasi, *RazFe,* 173 [1966], 105-106).

23. Achilles Gagliardi, S.J. *Ad Patres ac Fratres Societatis Jesu de plena cognitione Instituti opusculum.* Namur: F. Douxfils, 1841. Pp. 102. (Various editions were prepared by J. Boero, S.J. New edition in Bruges, 1882, "diligenter recognita").

This is an incomplete work. It contains only two of a projected four parts. The first part treats of the end of the Society, the second, of the means. There should have followed a third part on its members and a fourth on its government. As he does with all his works, he

composes his commentary within the framework of the doctrine of the "Three Ways" of the spiritual life (see Ignacio Iparraguirre and André Derville, *Dictionnaire de
spiritualité*, VI, columns 53-64.

24. Pedro Ribadeneyra, S.J., *Tratado en el qual se da razón del
Instituto de la Religión de la Compañía de Jesús*. Madrid,
1605. Pp. 343; 2nd ed., Salamanca, Eugenio Gracia de
Honorato, 1733. Pp. 444. A Latin translation by Laurent
Carli, S.J., was published in Rome in 1864.

Ribadeneyra explains and defends the special and novel
elements of the Institute, such as the suppression of a
special habit and of choir, special formation, the ap-
pointing of superiors, and the like. In this work, Ribadeneyra uses a different approach from that in his other
publications, He is not interested here in narrating what
he has seen and giving testimony about it; rather, he seeks
to show the juridical foundation of the Institute in the
light of the common law and that of other orders. See Ignacio Gordón, S.J., *Valores canónicos del P. Ribadeneira.
El tratado sobre el Instituto de la Compañía de Jesús*.
Granada: Facultad teoligica S.J., 1952. Pp. 70.

25. Julius Negrone, S.J. *Regulae communes Societatis Jesu com-
mentariis asceticis illustratae*. Milan: Pacifici et Io.
Bapt. Piccalei, 1613. Pp. 807. Modern edition: Aug. Arndt,
S.J., 4 vols. Krakow: Kozianski, 1913-1915. Pp. 374, 702,
490, 596.

26. Franciscus Suárez, S.J., *Tractatus de religione Societatis Jesu*.
Lyons, 1625; Moguntiae, 1626; Lyons, 1634: Venice, 1744;
Brussels-Paris, 1858; Paris, 1866.

This is treatise X of volume IV, *De virtute et statu
religionis*. It treats of the Institute in general, the
vows, studies, the means of perfection, ministries, government, and dismissal. It offers the theological foun-

dations of the principal elements. Suárez depends on Ribadeneyra. See Miguel Nicolau, S.J., in *Manresa,* 21 (1949), 121-138, especially 134-137.

27. Joannes Dirckinck, S.J., *Exhortationes ad religiosos.* Cologne: Godefridi Meucheri, 1704. Pp. 675. There are many editions. A modern edition is: August Lehmkuhl, S.J., 3 vols. Bruges: Beyaert, 1913. Pp. xv + 485; viii + 494; viii + 478.

This is a commentary on the *Summary of the Constitutions.* The value does not consist so much in his interpretation of the rules, in which he depends on Mannaerts (Manaraeus), as in the spiritual doctrine which is scattered throughout. It can truly be said that he succeeds in developing a treatise on religious perfection.

B. *In the Restored Society*

28. José Manuel Aicardo, S.J. *Comentario a las Constituciones de la Compañía de Jesús.* 6 vols. Madrid: Blass y Cía., 1919-1932. Each volume is roughly a thousand pages.

This is an immense storehouse of documents relating to the early Society, almost all of which have been drawn from the MHSJ, but together with some others which show historically the meaning and purpose of the various prescriptions. Very detailed and practical indices. He does not follow the order of the Constitutions, but a different one which he considers to be the order of their internal logic: (1) The end of the Society and the means of acquiring the perfection of its members (vol. 1 and 2); (2) contents of each of the ten Parts of the Constitutions (vols. 3 and 4); (3) The Society as an Order: its name, members, government, and preservation (vols. 5 and 6). See Enrique del Portillo, S.J., in *AHSJ*, 2 (1933), 96-99.

29. Paul de Chastonay, S.J., *Die Satzungen des Jesuitenordens:*

Werden, Inhalt, Geistesart. Einsiedeln: Benziger, 1938.
Pp. 278. A translation by the author himself into French
is: *Les Constitutions de l'ordre des Jésuites: Leur genèse,
leur contenu, leur esprit.* Paris: Aubier, 1941. Pp. iv +
254.

This is a very precise and useful treatise on the
genesis, content, and spirit of the Constitutions, with a
modern view of the problems. Occasionally the results are
suggestive rather than objective.

30. Augustus Coemans, S.J. *Commentarium in Regulas Societatis Iesu
omnibus nostris communes: in Summarium Constitutionum, in
regulas communes, in regulas modestiae.* Rome: apud Oecono-
mum Generalem, 1938. Pp. xv + 404. There is an English
translation by Matthew Germing, S.J. (El Paso: Revista
Católica Press, 1942. Pp. xii + 395.

This is very analytic and particularized. The author
has a broad grasp of the various points of the Institute
and introduces a large series of texts, especially from
the fathers general.

31. Eduardus Fine, S.J. *Iuris regularis tum communis tum particu-
laris quo regitur Societas Iesu declaratio.* Prato: Giac-
chetti, 1909. Pp. xii + 1160.

This is a juridical commentary. The author customarily treats problems with great depth, basing himself on
the important theologians and canonists of his day.

32. Moritz Meschler, S.J. *Die Gesellschaft Jesu: Ihre Satzungen
und ihre Erfolge.* 1st and 2nd ed. Freiburg: Herder, 1911.
Pp. xi + 308. There is a French translation by Philippe
Mazoyer (Paris, Lethielleux, 1911, pp. 354); an Italian
translation by Giovanni Re, S.J., (Rome: La civiltà
cattolica, 1917, pp. 396; 2nd ed., *ibid.*, 1932, pp. 396).

This is an exposition which is apologetic in character.
It treats not only of the origin, end, and means of the

Society, but also of the ways in which the Society realizes its end in various fields. It does not take much account of the primary or primitive sources.

33. Antonio Oraá, S.J. *Explanación de las Reglas del Summario de las Constituciones de la Compañía de Jesús.* Madrid: Majisterio Español, 1949. Pp. 377. *Explanación de las Reglas Comunes y de la Modestia de la Compañía de Jesús. Ibid:* 1951. Pp. 240.

These books are an adaptation of Coemans with some additions from other commentaries.

34. Augustinus Oswald, S.J. *Commentarius in decem partes Constitutionum Societatis Iesu.* 3rd ed. Ruremonde: Roermondsche Stoomdrukkerij, 1902: Pp. xx + 771.

This is an ample commentary which interweaves many texts from the Institute.

35. Henricus Ramière, S.J. *Compendium Instituti S.I., Praepositorum Generalium responsis et auctorum sententiis illustratum.* Mimeographed. Vals, 1855; Toulouse, 1880. Revised and augmented edition by Jules Besson, S.J., Toulouse, 1896. Pp. 533.

The principal value of this work lies in the many replies of the Fathers General which it includes.

36. Xavier de Ravignan, S.J. *De l'existence de l'institut des Jésuites.* Paris: Poussielgue-Rusand, 1844. Pp. 166; 2nd ed., Brussels: Scepens, 1898. Pp. x + 166. Translated into German by K Reiching, (Schaffhausen: Hurter, 1844, pp. 114); into Spanish by Vicente Miguel y Florez, Pbo. (Valencia: D. B. Monfort, 1845); into Flemish by Theodorus Brouwer (Arnhem: Vermeulen, 1844, pp. 124); into Portuguese by António Osorio de Campos e Silva (Lisbon: 1845, pp. xvi + 159); and into English by Charles Seager (London: Charles Dolman, 1844, pp. 84).

This book is both a defense of and an apologia for the Institute. The work is directed towards a public that would be indifferent or even hostile to the Society. It presents the Exercises, the phases of formation of Jesuits, government, ordinary life, obedience, and missions. It is written in a forceful and skillful style.

37. Joannes Roothan, S.J. *Adhortationes Spirituales*, in his *Opera spiritualia*, edited by Ludovicus De Jonge, S.J. and Petrus Pirri, S.J. (Rome: Curia S.J., 1936), Vol. I, 326-422.

38. Arthur Vermeersch, S.J. *Miles Christi Jesu; le Sommaire des Constitutions médité*. Turnhout: Brepois, 1914. Pp. 802; 3rd ed., Ibid., 1933. Pp. 814. Translated into English by E. F. Erbacher, S.J. (El Paso: Revista católica Press, 1951, pp. 587; 3rd ed., Calicut, India: Xavier Press, 1960, pp. 604); into Italian, (Acireale: Tip. Orario delle Ferrovie, 1925, pp. 776).

This book consists of meditations on the *Summary of the Constitutions*. It proceeds by considering in each rule the literal sense, the spirit or central virtue, and various practical applications. It is inspired principally by the letters of the fathers general. It is skillful in probing into the depths of the spirit and mind of St. Ignatius. It has a great deal of unction.

Supplementary Note:

39. *Ignatiana: Nuntii de historia spiritualitatis S.J.* (Rome), has published a special issue (nos. 18-19, May, 1963) on the Constitutions. In this issue are to be found: a synthesis of important works of criticism on the ten parts of the Constitutions; an introduction by Father Antonio M. de Aldama on the manner of reading, studying, and meditating on the Constitutions; notes on the text of the Constitutions as a source of spiritual reading; a brief analysis

of Pedro Sánchez Céspedes on the spiritual structure of the Constitutions; a study of Giampiero Rovarino on the terminology of service in the Constitutions; suggestions for the study of the Constitutions; and testimonies of various authors from the sixteenth century in regard to the Constitutions.

PART III. MODERN STUDIES ON GENERAL ASPECTS

40. Together with explicit studies on the Constitutions, we indicate here other works which can help to a more complete under- standing of them, some of which will study the evolution of the Society, the genesis and development of its juridi- cal structures, or other circumstances which illuminate the work of Ignatius in his editorial work on the Consti- tutions.

41. Maurizio Costa, S.J. *Legge religiosa e Discernimento spirituale nelle Costituzioni della Compagnia di Gesù.* Brescia: Paideia, 1973. Pp. 444.

 The Constitutions can give the impression of being a mixture of spiritual counsels and legal prescriptions, but a more profound analysis of their nature shows that they are the result of discernment over the various experiences of the many realities which occurred in the early Society; and that, consequently, the Constitutions furnish to su- periors the most suitable instrument they have for discern- ing the various situations which confront them.

 Though this work examines principally Part X of the Constitutions, by this means the essence of the other parts is also distilled and clarified. Part X is considered as both the climax and the synthesis of the Constitutions.

 The internal dynamism of the Constitutions moves in an alternating rythm: from experience to the letter and from the letter to experience. The text as it comes to us crystallizes the results of the experiences. And so, to interpret the thrust of the letter rightly, one must re-create for himself the original experience or reenact it. The light which best illumines this discretionary interpretation is that which comes from the Election of the Exercises. And so the Jesuit must put himself in the situation of making an election in order to be able to apply the Constitutions to the various situation of his life.

42. Michel Dortel-Claudot, S.J. *Le genre de vie extérieur de la Compagnie de Jésus*, Rome: Gregorian University Press, 1971. P*.* 73.

The author analyzes the meaning of that expression of the Formula of the Institute of 1550 that we are to follow "the common and approved usage of reputable priests" (*honestorum sacerdotum communem et approbatum usum*), a norm which was clear enough for the first Jesuits who used it frequently. It corresponds to a manner of expression which escapes us today. Dortel-Claudot aims to illuminate this meaning by highlighting its background, "ce langage, cet arrière-fond linguistique" (p. 126). To this end, he examines the significance that the words: "sacerdos, clericus, frater honestus" had from the 12th to the 16th centuries.

His conclusion is that this term was used to designate priests who are "conformed to canonical rules" (p. 37), "worthy and good-mannered . . . by their dress . . . and their respect for the norms of social propriety" (p. 47), "modest" by reason of "their moderation and discretion in speech, . . . discipline and custody of the senses, . . . propriety of gait" (pp. 47-49); "one who knows how to take account of those about him, adjust himself to circumstances, places, and persons, and who thereby manifests his respect for others" (p. 59). See François Courel in *RAM*, 47 (1971), 226-227.

Similar is the treatment in Dortel-Claudot, *Mode de view: Niveau de vie et pauvreté de la Compagnie de Jésus* (Rome: Centrum Ignatianum Spiritualitatis, 1973; pp. vii + 116).

43. Miguel Angel Fiorito, S.J. "Alianza biblica y regla religiosa: Estudio histórico-salvífico de las Constituciones de la Compañía de Jesús." *Stromata*, 21 (1965), 291-324.

Father Fiorito proceeds to demonstrate the importance of the biblical Covenant in the history of salvation, and

also the message of salvation which the phrases of this
Covenant contain. He does this in the light of those juridical expressions which portray the acts of extra-biblical
authorities. A religious vocation is interpreted as a special instance within the biblical Covenant. In each age of
the Church Christ raises up founders of religious orders
who re-incarnate this biblical Covenant in new formulae.

St. Ignatius was one of these founders. He always
understood himself to be an instrument of Christ, who was
the true founder of the Society. The juridical documents
in which the foundational charism of the Society is formulated possess the same characteristics as the expressions
of the biblical Covenant. Consequently, "the sole exact
interpretation of a vocation and of a religious rule is
that in terms of salvation history or, in other words,
that which reads the written document in the light of the
spiritual experience of the founder and legislator. The
religious rule aims not merely to provide an abstract norm,
but to provoke this same concrete salvific experience" (p.
320). Nevertheless, "the religious rule . . . is never to
be left isolated in that moment of salvation history which
gave it its rise, but must always remain open to new salvific experiences within the one and the same history of
salvation" (p. 321).

44. Maurice Giuliani, S.J. "Compagnons de Jésus", in *Christus* 6
(1959), no. 22, 221-239, and pp. 159-175 in *Prière et action:
Etudes de spiritualité ignatienne,* La Collection Christus
no. 21 (Paris: Desclée de Brouwer, 1966).

The full ideal of St. Ignatius is to be realized only
in the social form of companionship (*compagnonnage*). After
the first attempts, there was formed a community based on
fraternal love, oriented towards one ideal of action, ani-
mated by the same spirit, by an interior movement of the
Holy Spirit which guided all to the same line of conduct.
In this intimate compenetration is reflected the reciprocal

love of the Father and of the Son; in its apostolic ideal
is revealed the redemptive design of the Trinity; and in
its community is manifested the power which the Holy Spirit
receives from the Father and from the Son.

45. Jesús M. Granero, S.J. "De indole religiosa et apostolica So-
cietatis et de eius servitio in Ecclesia." Pp. 120-133 in
Documenta selecta Congregationis Generalis XXXI. Rome:
Centrum Ignatianum Spiritualitatis, 1973.

After considering the deficiencies which might have
restricted apostolic efficienty and the requirements of
accommodation, the author indicates these basic elements:
The Society of Jesus is a religious Institute of apostolic
inspiration, bound by special obedience to the pope and by
a subordinated religious obedience, with a universalistic
orientation. It is a clerical Institute inserted into the
Church, with the mission of spreading the Kingdom of Christ
with a defined orientation which is at the base of the
criteria of selection, in union with other apostolic forces.
It seeks its goals by means of community life, and under
the direction of the superior.

46. Heinrich Krauss, S.J. "Demokratie in der Gesellschaft Jesu?
Gedanken zum Verhältnis von Autorität und Gemeinschaft."
Geist und Leben, 41 (1968), 443-462.

The structures of the Society which refer to obedience
and to authority are based on the sixteenth-century sociological conception which is today viewed with skepticism.
Today there is a desire for democratization of government
in all its parts. The author asks if it is possible to
harmonize these desires in order to give to the Society a
more democratic form with a genuinely Ignatian mentality.
He proposes, merely as a working hypothesis, various ways
in which this might be done: by giving more power to provincial congregations, by a more efficient structuring of
consultations and community deliberations, by greater

sharing of the ordinary members in the resolution of the
chief problems, by a more decentralized jurisdiction, by
the attribution of a greater deliberative value to pro-
posals of all.

47. Michel Ledrus, S.J. *L'operosità della Compagnia*. Messina:
Ignatianum, 1968. Pp. 72.

This book consists of five conferences on five points
of the Institute of the Society: the help of souls; the
end and raison d'être of the Institute; evangelical mobility as characteristic of the Jesuit method of proceed-
ing; the obedience of the apostle, i.e., mobility directed
by a higher source which confers the character of mission;
evangelical obedience in its immediate ordering to Christ
as the key of organization for the ministry; insertion into
the Church by means of an organic ecclesial ratification
together with direct dependence on the Supreme Pontiff.

See also, by the same Michel Ledrus, S.J., *Temi di
esercizi spirituali* (Rome: Centrum Ignatianum, 1972), which
is available also in French: *Thèmes pour les Exercices
spirituels* (ibid.), wherein he continues his consideration
of some aspects of the Constitutions in the light of the
Exercises.

48. Francisco Javier Osuna, S.J. *"Amigos en el Señor": Estudio
sobre la génesis de la Comunidad en la Compañía de Jesús,
desde la conversión de san Ignacio (1521) hasta su muerte
(1556).* (Rome, Centrum Ignatianum, 1971, pp. 185).

St. Igantius succeeded in forming a community of
friends in the Lord who felt themselves united by an interior bond of love and a similar manner of procedure.
The community progressively defined itself and came to
such a maturity as to be constituted a religious order.
Its apostolic character became the community's reason for
existence and conditioned its style. These friends sought
to reproduce the life of Christ and of the apostles. The

community advanced by structuring itself especially on a
basis of communal deliberations in a climate of Ignatian
indifference. Through prayer, abnegation, and a frank
exchange of ideas they customarily arrived at a common
accord. Their joining together in the Eucharistic sacri-
fice formed the culminating moment of their prayer. This
communal gestation, which can be traced in the first legislative documents, in which the first diversification
already appears, illumines the legislation of the Constitutions regarding community life. The author treats of
this in the second part of his thesis which has not yet
been published.

49. Francisco Javier Osuna, S.J. "La Vida de comunidad en la
    primitiva Compañía hasta 1540 y en las Constituciones."
    Boletín del Centro de espiritualidad (Buenos Aires), no.
    11 (1971), 29-38.

    Osuna presents here a synthesis of his complete work,
and not just of the first part which was published as indicated in the preceding number.

    Here we indicate his conclusions in the still unpub-
lished second part. The community of fraternal friendship
and apostolic projects continued to develop and found faithful and protective expression in the Constitutions. The
essential nucleus of the Ignatian community is a community
conceived in function of apostolic mission, that is, a
group in which the concepts of community and of itinerant
apostolic mission are integrated. The apostolate is the
determining factor for the life-style of the community.
Community life is not the principle means envisaged by
the Constitutions for forming community. The bonds of
community should serve to unite members who are geograph-
ically separated: mutual love, frequent communication,
obedience, union, a sense of belonging to the whole body.
The Constitutions envisage the whole body of the Society
as *one* community. Common life signifies, within that

community, a suitable style of common simplicity lived by
all, but differentiated in regard to individuals according
to the needs of discreet charity and, in addition, by a
form of life which is common exteriorly but adapted to the
requirements of the region which is being evangelized.
The Society's sprituality which is described in Part VI
is presented in a communitarian perspective for an apostolic community of this kind.

50. François Roustang, "Le corps de la Compagnie." *Christus,* no.
13 (1966), 332-345.

The Constitutions point out the manner in which the
Jesuit will become progressively integrated into the body
of the Society, and through this, into humanity itself.
This fulness, united to the complexity of objectives which
are mingled together, explains why the Society is, on one
hand, one of the most structured of societies and, on the
other, one of the most difficult to capture in formulae.
The Society is, in its deepest reality, a body which per-
fects itself and achieves its growth through a dynamic
tension towards the end for which it was founded.

51. Manuel Ruiz Jurado, S.J. "Ejercicios y Constituciones."
Manresa, 43 (1971), 149-166.

Between the Exercises and the Constitutions there
are both many affinities and great dissimilarities. The
Exercises are a method which serves for any ecclesial
vocation; the Constitutions are for Jesuits. But in spite
of this basic difference, there is a special affinity which
derives "from the similarity between (1) the grace of vocation and the spiritual inclinations of those called to
the Society and (2) those of the author of the Spiritual
Exercises" (p. 151).

Father Ruiz Jurado proceeds to study the features of
the Exercises which have passed into the Constitutions
and the manner in which St. Ignatius has adjusted them.

On this same theme, see Arturo Codina, "Los Ejercicios . . .
y las Constituciones," *Manresa*, 8 (1932), 133-147.

52. Ignacio Salvat, S.J., *Servir en Misión: Aportación al estudio
del carisma de Ignacio de Loyola y de la Compañía de Jesús.*
Rome: Centrum Ignatianum Spiritualitatis, 1972. Pp. 186.

    Salvat first studies the evolution of the concept of
mission in the course of St. Ignatius' life, and then the
same concept of mission, its relation to the end of the
Society of Jesus, and to the entire structure of the Society.

    Everything in the Constitutions revolves around mis-
sion. The structures which the saint has chosen are in
function of this. The characteristics of government, the
principles of admission and formation of its members are
only two examples of the manner in which Ignatius kept
seeking for juridical ways to concretize this in the most
suitable way possible, so as to endow the Society with the
greatest possible mobility. The special vow of obedience
to the supreme pontiff is the foundation, and the other
specific elements are the means of continuing this mission-
ary spirit of the founders.

53. José Luis Urrutia, S.J. "Régimen de las Ordenes religiosas a
mediados del siglo XVI y aportación de san Ignacio."
Miscelánea Comillas, no. 36 (1961). Pp. 91-142.

    The author brackets the legislation of Ignatius within
the juridical mentality of his epoch. He studies what Ignatius included from the structures of religious orders of
the time and what he introduced himself as original elements. See also *RAM*, 39 (1963), 226-232.

54. John H. Wright, S.J., "The Grace of Our Founder and the Grace
of Our Vocation." *Studies in the Spirituality of Jesuits*,
3 (1971), 1-32. St. Louis: The American Assistancy Seminar
on Jesuit Spirituality. There is a Spanish translation:

"La gracia de nuestro fundador y la gracia de nuestra
vocación." *Boletín del centro de espiritualidad,* no. 12
(Buenos Aires: July, 1971, 24 pages).

Ignatius was, above all, a companion of Christ, one
who sought to penetrate into the mentality and spirit of
Christ in order to reproduce it. The contemplation of
Christ by this profound method, as it brought him closer
to him and made him more eager to realize this goal, also
made him a contemplative in action. The theological source
of this interior attitude is none other than the Holy Trinity itself. To live as the companion of Christ was for
Ignatius to live as the son of God the Father, under the
inspiration of the Holy Spirit. The objective was to
serve the Church and to transform the world. The means
was the Society of Jesus, that is, a priestly community,
endowed with mobility, which was to be somewhat a repro-
duction in itself of the apostolic college which was the
first "Society of Jesus."

PART IV. STUDIES ON PARTICULAR POINTS

A. *Principles of Interpretation for the Constitutions*

55. Maurizio Costa, S.J., and Ignacio Iparraguirre, S.J. "Genere
    letterario ed ermeneutico delle Costituzioni." Pages 97-
    119 in *Dossier Constitutiones A,* (on which see no. 1 above).

    The Constitutions are a document pertaining to the
    founding of the Society. They arose from reflection on
    experience, and they are preserved in the same manner.
    They are not only the result of discernment but also an
    instrument for it. Further still, they are the key docu-
    ment of spiritual discernment for the preservation and
    development of the Society. From these considerations are
    derived the attitudes and basic norms which Father Costa
    develops (pp. 102-108).

    Furthermore, one must take into account their environ-
    mental spiritual attitude, the basic presupposition of
    judging everything according to the principles of the Ex-
    ercises, the theological and spiritual foundation, the
    scope of the literal statement and the heterogenity of its
    elements. Intermingled in any paragraph of the Constitu-
    tions are the purpose of a given prescription, the spiritual
    principles on which it is based, the attitude to be main-
    tained in respect to it, the concrete situation in which
    the Jesuit may find himself, the content, the means, and
    the particular method of putting themselves into execution.
    Discernment must proceed by validating each one of the el-
    ements in order to avoid an unreasonable literalness or an
    uncontrolled liberty. It is highly important to view the
    prescriptions of minute details in relation to the function
    and finality of the Constitutions as a whole (p. 113).

56. Miguel Angel Fiorito, S.J. "Contribución a la interpretación
    de las Constituciones." Pp. 275-284 in *Dossier "Consti-
    tutiones" A* (no. 1 above).

This essay indicates three distinctions that St. Ignatius makes: (1) between execution and consideration; (2)
between intention and execution, and (3) between the more
universal and summary Constitutions and the Declarations
about them.

Then the author presents three principles of interpretation: (1) all that the Constitutions have to say regarding the end or ends should be normative for the interpretation of the means, and not vice-versa; (2) what they
state more universally should be the norm of interpretation
for what they state more particularly; and (3) all that is
said in the Constitutions more briefly, because it is less
clear at one first reading, becomes richer through an interpretative reading or repeated interpretative readings.

Thereupon the author applies these three principles
to the themes of the end of the Society, and of the Society
as a body. He includes three appendices, (1) on fixed revenues; (2) on community life; (3) on the relationship between the Exercises and the Constitutions. He does this
(page 283) to enable us see how "beneath and within each
particular instance there is some universal: for example,
recourse to the "collateral associate" (*Constitutions*,
[659]) is justified as a particular institutionalization
for the case of a superior who does not possess all the
qualities necessary for his office; but in the "collateral"
is typified an attitude for every Jesuit to cultivate in
his local community, i.e., to be an "angel of peace" and
not an "author of division" (*Constitutions*, [664]).

57. George E. Ganss, S.J. "St. Ignatius' Personal Charism and Its
Institutionalization in His *Constitutions*," pages 131-140
in *Dossier "Constitutions"* A (no. 1 above).

Usually every religious founder, like a poet, has
charismatic ideals or inspirations which he tries to ex-
press in his legislation. But it always falls somewhat
short of the ideals. The legislated structures sometimes

cramp the members' charismatic spontaneity; but without
the structures the charism itself vanishes. Often, too,
among the ideals are conflicts or seeds of tension which
come to light only five, ten, or more years later.

For example, Ignatius wove together in his Constitutions his inspiring ends, such as "greater praise, glory,
or service of God" (*Cons*, [603, 609, 622, 693]) and prescriptions of minute details characteristic of his own era,
such as requiring scholastics to attend clases in pairs
(ibid., [349])--details which often puzzle or irritate us
today. But all these details are means to his subordinate
ends, and they in turn to his supreme yet simple end and
norm of choice: greater glory to God. By looking chiefly
to his ends in his single statutes, and especially to his
supreme end, we have a principle of interpretation helpful
toward separating the perennial elements in his Constitutions from those merely timely.

As another example, an inspiring ideal of 1540 was
expressed in *Cons*, [324, 588, 603, 618]: the professed
were to be kept free for missions, usually of two or three
months (ibid., [615]), from the pope or general. Often,
however, as experience showed, the good achieved on missions of short duration turned out to be short-lived.
Meanwhile another ideal was advancing toward clearer for-
mulation, the norm for choosing ministries: the greater
service of God and the more universal, long-lasting good
(ibid., [618, with Declaration D in 622,a]), such as
that being obtained through colleges and universities
(ibid.,[622,e]); and this more universal good usually
required much stability. Thus a conflict was set up between mobility and stability, and it has existed ever
since. The two ideals are in a healthy tension. They
are like two opposite guy ropes which support a pole.
If either grows too strong and unchecked by the other,
it topples the pole and both ropes with it. Each Jesuit,
when caught in the tension between the two ideals, must

apply anew the norm of choice: Which procedure is likely
to result in greater glory to God?

B. *The Name of the Society of Jesus (Compañía de Jesús,
    Societas Jesu)*

58. Theodor Baumann, S.J., "Compagnie de Jésus. Origine et sens
     primitif de ce nom." *RAM*, 37 (1961), 47-60.

    Polanco, Mannaerts, and Nadal give a military signif-
icance to the word *Compañía* in the title of the Society.
But for St. Ignatius, this word held the ordinary signif-
icance of a gathering of companions, whether stable or
occasional. (See in Monumenta Ignatiana, *Fontes narrativi*,
I, 452: "a woman who was of the group [*compañía*].") When
Ignatius associates the word *compañía* with Jesus, he signifies "companions of Jesus," united very closely to Jesus.
There is also an intimate relationship between the mystical
experiences of the felt presence of Jesus and the expression
Compañía de Jesús (on this see also below, 59 and 60). St.
Theresa uses the word *compañía* five times to indicate the
proximity of the human nature of Christ. It can therefore
be affirmed that the primitive meaning of *Compañía de Jesús*
is simply that of "companions of Jesus."

59. Theodor Baumann, S.J., "Compagnie de Jesus. La confirmation de
     ce nom dans la vision de la Storta." *RAM*, 38 (1962), 52-
     63.

    The vision of La Storta is closely related to the
name Society of Jesus (*Compañía de Jesús, Societas Jesu*).
In it the mystical experiences, the ideals which had mo-
tivated the life of Ignatius were centered in a fixed
manner on Rome and polarized toward the concrete work of
the Society. What he had been so anxious to find in the
Holy Land he found at the gates of Rome. His desire to
serve Christ in abjection and poverty, which he had thought
to realize in the Holy Land, was going to be realized with
his companions in Rome. Thus he already glimpsed somewhat

the founding of the Society. He felt himself officially
associated with the Son by the Father. They were already
the companions of Jesus.

60. Jesús Iturrioz, S.J., "Compañía de Jesús: Sentido histórico y
ascético de este nombre", *Manresa*, 27 (1955), 43-53. He
shows how the Italian word *Compagnia* designated in the
ecclsiastical language of the period a pious association
for the furtherance of good works or of worship.

61. "The title *Compañía de Jesús*," pages 345-349 in G. E. Ganss'
translation of the Constitutions (on which see no. 11 above).
St. Ignatius and his companions used the word *Compañía*
as found in the Society's title in many senses and with
varying implications or connotations, e.g., a group, group
of friends or companions, or a military group. When using
Latin, they habitually translated *Compañía*, not by *sodalitas*,
sodalitium, or *amicitia*, but by *Societas*, which implied or
connoted also juridical bonds and not merely companionship.
Throughout the Constitutions Ignatius used *Compañía de
Jesús* as the title of his order; and the title approved by
the Church, in *Regimini* of 1540 and later, is *Societas Iesu*.
Ignatius' mature meaning and ideal appear in *Constitutions*,
[655, 659, 662, 668, 871, 873, 821]. To try today to
select some one meaning as the simple or only meaning is
to oversimplify the problems connected with this topic.
The many meanings reciprocally enrich one another.

C. *The End of the Society*

62. François Courel, S.J., "La fin unique de la Compagnie de Jésus."
AHSJ, 35 (1966), 186-211.
The end of the Society is not two-fold, as might appear at first glance from the fact that the various elements which compose it are united in the Constitutions
with the copulative "and": service of God *and* help of the

neighbor. He adds that the larger part of the apostolic religious orders of the 16th Century had two ends.

But in the Formula of the Institute there is mention of only one end, in the singular. The more detailed analysis of the Ignatian texts leads to the same conclusion. The glory of God and the service of the neighbor form one single end. All the rest, including one's own perfection, are only means, even if essential means, to the accomplishment of this end. The guiding idea in the founding of the Society is the search for the glory of God in all things.

63. See also, in regard to the end of the Society, the *Exhortationes* of Laynez, 2nd exhortation, pages 139-143 of no. 66 below.

64. By the way of complement, see also the bibliography on Ignatius the legislator, in *OrientBibliograf*, nos. 194-195; and also on the history of the founding of the Society. On this latter topic, see also the study of Antonio Jimenez Oñate, *El origen de la Compañía de Jésus. Carisma fundacional y génesis histórica*, (Rome, 1966, pp. xviii + 193. Bibliotheca Instituti Historici S.I., no. 25), which traces the course of the founding from the seed of Manresa to the full flowering.

D. *The Ancient Preface of the Constitutions*

65. François Courel, S.J. "De praefatione antiqua Constitutionum." *AHSJ*, 34 (1965), 253-257.

The first edition of the Constitutions (1559) had as a preface (*Praefatio*) a synthesis of the Institute of the Society. Responsibility for this preface has come to be attributed to Pedro de Ribadeneyra. But there is no document prior to the 2nd edition of the Life of St. Ignatius by Bartoli, published in 1659, which bears out this tradition. This evidence is not very convincing, both because it is so late and also because Bartoli changed his

own opinion. In the first edition, he attributed responsibility to Nadal for this preface; and he returned to
this same opinion in his Latin edition of 1605.

These fluctuations of Bartoli take the strength out
of his affirmation. It should also be noted that he does
not take the text directly from the printed edition of the
Constitutions, but from Sacchini, and it does not agree in
all details with the text published in 1559.

E. The General Examen

66. Cándido de Dalmases, S.J. "Le esortazioni del P. Lainex sull'
Examen Constitutionum." *AHSJ*, 35 (1966), 132-185.

This is the publication of the integral text of six-
teen exhortations which Laynez, then general of the Society,
gave in 1559 to the Jesuits in Rome. Laynez explains various important points of the Institute: the name and end
of the Society, the vows, grades, admission and dismissal,
the novitiate, and other themes which are proposed to candidates at the time of their entrance into the Society.

F. Apostolic Activity

67. Gustave Martelet, S.J. "Naturaleza de la única vocación apostólica en la Compañía." Pp. 91-98 in *Congreso Internacional
de Hermanos*. Rome: Centrum Ignatianum Spiritualitatis, 1971.

The Society, as part of the Church, shares in its salvific mission. The Society places itself at the service
of Christ and, grafted onto the Church, receives its divine
apostolic mandate. It seeks to realize this misssion with
the fullness which only the ministerial priesthood offers.
For the sake of more effective action, it unites in a vital
and organic manner members who are not priests with those
who can realize its function as a priestly body.

The brothers, consecrated to God apostolically in a
priestly body, are religious apostles. They find their

relationship to the priesthood through their intimate insertion into the body of the Society. They are not priests
personally, but fraternally.

68. Miguel Mendizábal, S.J. *Algunas notas visibiles del operario
evangelico, subrayadas en el epistolario ignaciano.* Rome:
Gregorian University, 1969. Pp. 48.

This study deals with directives given by St. Ignatius
to Jesuit workers as these revolve about a series of vir-
tues. This fascicle forms part of a doctoral thesis in
which is analyzed the example of a life in humility and
lowliness as a realization of hope and confidence in God,
as is also the case with poverty. But Mendizábal has published only the first chapter of his thesis in which are
treated the directives of Ignatius on the example of life.

G. *The Temporal Coadjutors*

69. José Benitez. *Coadjutores temporales. Comentario al Decreto
no. 7 de la Congregación General XXXI de los coadjutores
temporales.* Quito, 1969.

The author endeavors to prove that for St. Ignatius,
the term and the structure of temporal coadjutors is different from the traditional understanding of "lay brothers."
The coadjutor is a collaborator and cooperator in the apostolate. According to his qualifications and the needs of
the Society, he can pursue every kind of study and ministry,
including non-priestly spiritual ministries. The term means
essentially a complement of a primary and apostolic activity,
as an active member who participates in the work and in its
responsibilities. It is opposed, not to "priest," but to
"professed."

"Temporal" does not signify simply non-spiritual, but
implies a much fuller content of action closed to priests
insofar as it would not be appropriate to them. The unity
of vocation demands that within it there be specific func-

tions for each one of its categories. The temporal function, necessary for the efficiency of the order, has to be realized by the coadjutors, not because they cannot do other things, but because in this fashion they realize their own special mission.

70. Carlos M. De Melo, S.J. "La mente de san Ignacio acerca del oficio especial de los hermanos coadjutores: 'para ayudar en las cosas exteriores o temporales." Pp. 156-163 in *Congreso internacional* (above, no. 67).

Temporal coadjutors form a single grade with spiritual coadjutors. They are not clerics, but they are true religious, apostles, they should be selected, and well-tested. They need not have studied. Their specific end is to help and assist the Society in necessary exterior things, especially in domestic concerns, but they are not excluded from being occupied with more lofty affairs.

In the entire question of coadjutor brothers, care must be taken to distinguish between principles established by St. Ignatius in the Constitutions, and their concrete application as practiced from the beginning of the Society to a concrete situation in the socio-historical context of the sixteenth century.

71. Miguel Angel Fiorito, S.J., "Las actividades apostólicas que no requieren el orden sagrado," pages 191-198 in *Congreso internacional* (no. 67 above).

Fiorito outlines, on the basis of a careful analysis of Ignatian texts, "the apostolic image of the brother which is charted between two guideposts: negatively, what does not require sacred orders, positively, what follows from our common priesthood, from apostolic religious consecration, and from the apostolic end of the Society as a body" (p. 191).

Granted that the ministries which, as a matter of fact, the brother can exercise are conditioned by socio-cultural circumstances, Fiorito rises above concrete applications so

as to establish Ignatian criteria which should govern this
application, according to various eras.

72. Jesús M. Granero, S.J. "Los hermanos coadjutores." *Manresa*,
44 (1972), 5-24.

On the basis of the primitive documents, Granero
studies the way in which coadjutor brothers came into being,
their raison d'être, the nature of their vows, the distinction between coadjutors who are "formed" and those who are
"not formed," the duties of the coadjutors which, for our
author, are "temporal and domestic occupations" (p. 18).

73. Aloys Grillmayer, S.J., "Concepto teológico de la vocación
religiosa y apostólica de los HH. coadjutores de la Compañía de Jesús." Pp. 99-155 in *Congreso internacional*
(no. 67 above).

This examines, on the basis of the teaching of Vatican
Council II, the figure of the lay religious. Hence, the
present work is not a study on the coadjutor brothers according to the Constitutions, but we think it is very useful for situating the vocation of the brother within an
ecclesial and theological context. Grillmayer proceeds
by the theology of the "common priesthood," of the religious
state in so far as it is "religious," and of the work in a
world created by God with its anthropological projection
in the sociological and ecclesiastical context of today.
He concludes by indicating the traits which should char-
acterize the new image of the brother in the Society of
Jesus.

74. Ignacio Iparraguirre, S.J. "Formación de los Hermanos en la
antigua Compañía", in *Congreso internacional* (no. 67
above), pp. 230-241.

The manner of forming brothers is helpful toward a
better understanding of the meaning of the Constitutions
in their references to the life and spirituality of the

coadjutor brother--supposing, of course, that the paradigm
of the Constitutions for the brothers' formation is followed.

75. Estanislao Olivares, S.J. "Los coadjutores espirituales y
temporales de la Compañía de Jesús. Su origen y sus votos."
AHSJ, 33 (1964), 102-119.

Admission into the Society was granted to some who
wanted to serve God in a more simple way than the professed.
These, at the beginning, were limited to taking private vows.
Desiring to give a juridical form to this institution, Ignatius consulted an official of the Curia. Among the solutions offered, he chose the form of the simple conditioned
vows, for the time that the Society would desire to retain
these members. These vows were still private vows. But he
was not entirely satisfied with this formula. In the Constitutions of 1549 the vows already appear as public. This
evolution was completed between the years 1548 and 1549.
During the life of Ignatius there were four spiritual coadjutors and twelve temporal coadjutors who pronounced vows
which were juridically public.

76. Worthy of consultation, too, is Michel Dortel-Claudot, "Frères
coadjuteurs jésuites," in *Dictionnaire de spiritualité*,
V, columns 1217-1221.

8. *The Colleges*

77. Lazslo Lukács, S.J. "De origine collegiorum externorum deque
controversiis circa eorum paupertatem obortis, 1539-1608."
Part I, 1539-1556, is in *AHSJ*, 29 (1960), 189-245; Part II,
on the later developments, 1556-1608, ibid., 30 (1961),
3-89.

In the beginning, the Society possessed neither colleges nor its own centers of formation. Those who entered
underwent their formation in various universities. Only

when the number of those being incorporated into the Society was increasing did classes begin to be held in some
university centers. Classes were begun in Gandía in 1546
and in Messina in 1548. In this manner the first colleges
for young Jesuits arose. Each time more students who were
not Jesuits were admitted into them. Father Lukács makes
a statistical study of all these colleges: the number of
professors, of students, of Jesuits and lay students in
each college.

The Constitutions incorporated explicitly the two
early types of colleges, those for young Jesuits exclusively and those principallly for Jesuits but with some lay
students; and only implicitly the last type, colleges
primarily for lay students.

78. A full summary of the above article in 27 pages is given in
Didattica, no. 102 (Rome: March, 1963). An English digest
is that by George E. Ganss, S.J., "The Origin of Jesuit
Colleges for Externs and the Controversies about their
Poverty, 1539-1608," *Woodstock Letters*, 91 (1962), 123-
161. See also Ignacio Iparraguirre, S.J., "Pensamiento
y actitud de san Ignacio de Loyola acerca de los colegios",
Revista calasancia, 31 (1962), 189-198.

I. *Community: Common Life*

79. John C. Futrell, S.J. *Making an Apostolic Community of Love:
The Role of the Superior according to St. Ignatius of
Loyola*. St. Louis: The Institute of Jesuit Sources, 1970.
Pp. vii + 231.

St. Ignatius formed a community of love. The superior
was its animator. The structure of governing was integrated
into this concept of love which is itself a reflection of
the love that God has, in his providence, for all men.
Without this note, the function of the superior is deformed
and the concept of Ignatian community is adulterated.

The superior must be a man who knows how to achieve
spiritual discernment of a concrete situation, that is,
how to evaluate, during the communitarian search for God's
will, the others' (1) opinions founded on appearances,
(2) their more deeply felt concepts, and (3) their deci-
sions; and above all, how to form an apostolic community
of love in which all the members help one another in the
service of Christ, by uniting the members among themselves
and stimulating their apostolic activity. For reviews,
see: V. C. in *Selecciones de libros s. fco. de borja*, 9
(1972), 446–447; F. Courel, S.J., in *RAM*, 47 (1971), 226–
227; P. De Letter, S.J., in *African Ecclesiastical Review*,
15 (1972), 182–183; P. De Letter, S.J., in *The Clergy
Monthly*, 35 (August, 1971), 314–315; J. M. Granero, S.J.,
in *Manresa*, 43 (1971), 225–227; J. D. Keller, O.S.A., in
Review for Religious, 30 (1971), 720–721; A. Ravier, S.J.,
in *AHSJ*, 40 (1971), 486–487; L. Renard, S.J., in *Nouvelle
Revue Theologique*, 95 (1973), 1023–1024; Sister M. Xavier,
O.S.U., in *Sisters Today*, 42 (1971), 528–530; *The Way*, 11
(1971), 176–177.

J. *The General Congregation*

80. Jozef de Roeck, S.J. "Du sens de la Congrégation général dans
     la Compagnie de Jésus d'après les Constitutions." *AHSJ*,
     35 (1966), 212–229.

     The general congregation is not reducible to a merely
juridical entity, but is rather the expression of the love
and universal union of the Society. This is the conclusion
of De Roeck after his analysis of Part VIII of the Constitutions in their various redactions and his examination
of the various problems which are treated therein: the
necessity, convocation and procedure of the general congregation, and participation in it.

81. Francisco Javier Egaña, S.J. *Orígines de la Congregación*

general en la Compañía de Jesús. Estudio histórico-jurídico de la octava parte de las Constituciones. Bibliotheca Instituti Historici S.J., no. 33. Rome: Institutum Historicum S.J., 1972. Pp. xxiv + 385.

Father Egaña studies the origins and development of procedure followed by St. Ignatius and his companions for the election of the general and the elaboration of legislation for the general congregation: the preliminary meetings, first written depositions, the various redactional stages of Part VIII of the Constitutions, and the various historical events which were interwoven into the holding of the First General Congregation.

The evolution developed in two phases: the charismatic, in which elements of a spontaneous nature predominated, comprised the first years. The second was extended through the whole time in which the various steps of the congregation were being systematized in the light of the Constitutions of older orders. The third, the juridical phase, took in the work of the congregation itself.

In the first phase, the purpose was to find the will of God in the matter with which the group was concerning itself: to make an election according to the tenor of the Exercises. In the second, it was to promote the personal union of the members. In the last, to resolve problems of government.

82. Ladislas Orsy, S.J. "Some Questions about the Purpose and Scope of the General Congregation." *Studies in the Spirituality of Jesuits,* 4 (1972), 85-114. St. Louis: The American Assistancy Seminar on Jesuit Spirituality, 1972.

For purposes of reflection and discussion, the author poses questions and some tentative answers, especially about the spirit and structures of a general congregation, what can reasonably be expected from the next one, and some practical suggestions toward improving the structures of general congregations.

83. John W. Padberg, S.J. "The General Congregations of the Society
of Jesus: A Brief Survey of Their History." *Studies in
the Spirituality of Jesuits,* 6 (1974), 1-127. St. Louis:
The American Assistancy Seminar on Jesuit Spirituality,
1974.

> Into this brief compass the author compresses and
documents the highlights of all the general congregations,
from I in 1558 through XXXI in 1955-1956. The progress
and procedures used in General Congregation XXXI are described extensively.

K. *The Account of Conscience*

84. Santiago de Goiri. *La apertura de conciencia en la espiritualidad de san Ignacio de Loyola.* Bilbao: Desclée de Brouwer,
1960. Pp. 403.

> A historical introduction examines the opening up of
conscience earlier than St. Ignatius. Then the first part
studies the opening up of conscience in St. Ignatius' personal spirituality; and the remaining parts examine how
this is realized in the Exercises, in the Constitutions,
and in the times after St. Ignatius' death.

> In the third part, which is what interests us here
more directly, the author indicates first the finality of
this openness in function of the end of the Society, greater
glory to God, the common good and the particular good of
the individual, and the paternal government of the superior.
Then he examines the General Examen in relation to the account of conscience, the matter of this account, the person
who should receive it, and the circumstances which should
accompany it.

85. V. Fecki. "Manifestatio conscientiae vigens in Societate Jesu."
Pages 71-101 in *De manifestatione conscientiae in iure
religiosorum* (Lublin, 1961).

> This work is predominantly juridical in character.

L. Communitarian Discernment and Deliberation

The major part of these studies analyzes the conception
and tactics of Ignatius in general or in the Exercises.
But because of the implications of this topic for the style
of obedience and of government in the Society, we think
it necessary to indicate them.

86. Various authors of the Province of Argentina. "La vida de
comunidad a la luz de los documentos ignacianos." Pages
61-87 in *Dossier "Deliberatio"* A. Rome: Centrum Ignatianum
Spiritualitatis, 1972. The names of the authors are listed
on p. 87.

In the light of Ignatian documents, the authors con-
clude that communitarian deliberation is one method of
finding the will of God in common, for it is a method of
being liberated in common from disordered affections, in
respect to a given community, through unanimity. The
method requires that there be basic agreement on the level
of their unity and orientation, so that disagreements exist
only in regard to the concrete means. It presupposes sin-
cerity and simplicity, flexibility, availability, indefinite
length of time, and reasoning pro and con by all. The authors apply these principles to concrete communities.

87. Antonio Baruffo, S.J. "Appunti per il discernimento e la
deliberazione in comune." Pages 133-156 in *"Dossier
"Deliberatio"* B. Rome, Centrum Ignatianum Spiritualitatis,
1972.

The author studies first the elements of discernment
and of deliberation in common in the spiritual tradition
of the Society and of the Church; that is, in the Exercises,
in the life-style of the first companions, in the Constitutions, and in Vatican Council II. He then goes on to
apply Ignatian principles to present-day practice.

88. Maurizio Costa, S.J. "Note sulla Deliberazione communitaria alla luce delle Costituzioni." Pages 295-331 in *Dossier, "Deliberatio" A*, (no. 86 above).

    To locate the problem within the general structure of the whole, the principal elements of Part VIII and of chapter 6 of Part IX are studied first, and the various modes of procedure in various kinds of communal deliberations are analyzed: the general congregation, recourse to definitors, and consultations. From this the author deduces the analogy of the concepts in the various circumstances, and especially the difference between discernment and deliberation. "Communal discernment" in the proper sense occurs when a group is performing: definitors with Father General, a conference of assistants, a general congregation. The concept is analogically verified when a personal discernment is made in relation to the community.

    In communitarian deliberation, a distinction should be made between the entire process of election and the culminating moment when the choice itself is made. In the general congregation, the deliberation is properly speaking communitarian whether it refers to the whole process or to the culminating moment. A truly communal election is achieved. On the other hand, in the ordinary government of the general, the entire process is communal, but not the culminating moment. The choice or decision is personal; but it can be called communal in an analogous sense, insofar as the work of a group has converged in the decision.

89. John Carroll Futrell, S.J. "Ignatian Discernment." *Studies in the Spirituality of Jesuits*, 2 (1970), 47-88. St. Louis: The American Assistancy Seminar on Jesuit Spirituality, 1970. A Spanish translation is in *Boletín del Centro de espiritualidad* (Buenos Aires), no. 8, 1-43.

There are also translations into French, Indonesian, Japanese, and Portuguese. Also, this work is on pages 19-60 of *Dossier "Deliberatio"* A (no. 87 above).

The author analyzes the various terms which St. Ignatius employs when he is describing discernment (*parecer, mirar, sentir, juzgar*), the structure of the Ignatian process of discernment, and the communal deliberation of the First Fathers. See also *Making an Apostolic Community of Love* (no. 79 above), chs. 5 and 6, pp. 106-156.

90. John Carroll Futrell has also published five other works on communal discernment in *Dossier "Deliberatio"* B, (no. 87 above), papers nos. 11-15, pp. 173-234.

He applies the Ignatian dynamism of election to present-day communities and clarifies the special characteristics of communal deliberation as illumined by the method followed by St. Ignatius and his first companions in the realization of their own communal discernment.

91. Piet Penning De Vries, S.J. *Ignatius of de spiritualiteit der Jesuïten*. Tielt-Den Haag: Lannoo, 1964. Pp. 200. A Spanish translation by Horacio Bojorge, S.J., is *Discernimiento: Dinámica existencial de la doctrina y del espíritu de san Ignacio de Loyola*. Espiritualidad ignaciana, no. 7. Bilbao: Mensajero, 1967. Pp. 224. An English version by W. Dudok van Heel is *Discernment of Spirits according to the Life and Teaching of St. Ignatius of Loyola*. Jericho, New York: Exposition Press, 1973. Pp. iv + 252.

Penning de Vries seeks to illumine from the life of Ignatius the profound meaning of discernment. He presents Ignatius as a man of the Exercises and of the Constitutions. On this basis, he describes the Ignatian dynamic of discernment. The author made a summary of his conclusions on pp. 135-144 of *Dossier "Deliberatio"* A (no. 86 above).

92. Michael Sheeran, S.J. "Discernment as a Political Problem. The Ignatian Art of Government." *Woodstock Letters,* 98 (1969), 446-464. Reproduced on pages 89-108 of *Dossier "Deliberatio"* A (no. 86 above).

The author first examines discernment in general, then communal discernment in particular as at the origin of the Society. Only through discernment did the First Fathers come to see the special structure of the Society. The renovation of structures will be accomplished in the same manner in which they were created. Discernment is the renewing element, the quintessence of Jesuit policy and style.

M. Jesuit Scholastics

93. Jesús M. Granero, S.J., "La Compañía de Jesús y sus estudiantes (1540 a 1556)." *Manresa*, 43 (1971), 5-46.

The author first studies the raison d'être of the scholastics, the way in which this grade developed, and the spiritual life that was proper to it. Mortification and the abnegation of one's own will held a great importance. So also did obedience, in which St. Ignatius would admit of no attenuation. The saint created an atmosphere in which the scholastics moved, and which offered them conditions suitable for living the religious spirit with great intensity. He continued to establish regulations suited to this purpose. And he was concerned to eliminate anything which might disturb study.

The type of studies pursued was determined in function of their specifically Jesuit purpose. The disciplines as found in the great universities were accepted. These corresponded to contemporary ecclesiastical studies. He sought to keep doctrine safe, by discouraging the use of suspect authors or books. Priestly ordination was normally deferred until after studies, so as to avoid the disruption that priestly ministries would bring to quiet and reflection necessary for study.

94. Estanislao Olivares, S.J. *Los votos de los escolares de la Compañía de Jesús: Su evolución jurídica.* Bibliotheca

Instituti historici S.I. no. 19. Rome: Institutum Historicum
S.J., 1961. Pp. 250.

The juridical status of the scholastic came to be
forged little by little. St. Ignatius, for some ten years,
tried various solutions: absolute vows of poverty and
chastity and a conditioned vow to enter the Society; a
single vow of entering the Society with permission to
add the three vows of religion; conditioned religious vows
plus the fourth, of entering the Society. This last became the definitive formula.

After this historical review, Olivares examines the
juridical nature of the vows in their definitive state
and the problematic to which they gave rise: On one side,
the vows were not accepted by the Society, and so were
not public vows, and on the other, Gregory XIII attributed
to them a public character. After examining more than 50
commentators, Olivares concludes that the vows of scholastics were religious but not public vows, recognized in
the Church as having a special juridical character.

N. Hope

95. Maurizio Costa, S.J. *Costituzioni e speranza. Scegliere la
speranza.* Rome: Ed. Stella Mattutina, 1973.

The experience which lies at the origin of the Constitutions, and so of their renewal, presupposes a climate
of hope. Only by hoping in the future can this experience
be realized. The author examines this vision of hope,
especially in Part X, the vital core of the Constitutions,
delaying on the first paragraph as the "heart" of the
entire part. Christ, who calls the Society into being
and directs it, is the ground for hope. Only the assimi-
lation of this reality can make possible our unconditional
response. The Jesuit is capable of experiencing an impulse
to commit himself only if he experiences himself as moved
by hope for the future. To realize this, he must make a

genuine discernment about the nature of this vocation and
see that Christ, who is always the same, will continue in
the future to choose his co-workers, as he has in the past.
All of this supposes, as its sine qua non, this opening
up of confidence in the future.

Such a confident perception demands a kind of education. One has to relive the stages of development of the
First Fathers and, like them, by trusting in the God who
directs the Society, to commit himself always more and
more. The experiments of the novitiate, especially in
the area of poverty, are the best education for this hope.
By means of hope, one comes to experience an impulse to
accomplish his mission and to use all his natural resources.
He sees in these the way in which God has made him capable
of cooperating with Himself.

96. Norbert Kotyla, S.J. *Ignatius von Loyola und die Gesellschaft
Jesu: Gottvertrauen für die Zukunft.* Rome: Gregorian
University Press, 1971. Pp. 88.

The way in which God had dealt with Ignatius "up to
the present" caused him to believe that God would continue
to help him in the future. The author treats of an intimate experience, felt in the deepest part of his being,
that God does direct the Society as "his very own." God
lacks neither the power nor the knowledge to carry his
works forward; and just as the Society is the work of God
and not that of Ignatius, since it is indeed the "Company
of Jesus," the Lord is almost "obliged" to supply contin-
ually what is lacking to Ignatius and to its superiors,
who are only instruments of God.

But God's carrying the enterprise forward does not
necessarily mean that it will enjoy human prosperity, nor
that it must always grow larger, nor even that it will be
preserved forever. Ignatius does not know what will happen, but he knows that, whatever happens, that which God
wills will be achieved. In the direction marked out by
God the cross always enters as an integral part; but it

is the cross as a means of salvation and of resurrection.

O. *The Grades*

97. Antonio M. Aldama, S.J. "De coadiutoribus in mente et in praxi Sancti Ignatii." *AHSJ*, 38 (1969), 389-430.

   After reviewing the evolution which gave rise to the institution of coadjutors, the author analyzes the Ignatian legislation in detail, in regard to the degree of union which the coadjutors had with the Society, the characteristics of their vocation, the qualities which they should possess. He analyzes the process of legislation as it moved through three periods: in 1546, before the arrival of Polanco; in 1547-1550, while Ignatius was preparing the new Formula of the Institute; and finally in the years 1551-1553, during which he wrote the definitive text of the Constitutions. The article ends with a study of Ignatius' practice in regard to the admission of coadjutors.

98. Jesús M. Granero. "Los profesos de la Compañía." *Manresa*, 42 (1970), 19-50.

   Ignatius' charism in founding the Society, "is a chain or complex of lights and movements which are crowned and completed only with the last moment of his life" (p. 20). The later graces complete the earlier ones. Granero shows how this charism in its earliest hours takes shape and develops into the differentiation of the members of the Society which culminates in the diversity of grades. He examines the reasons which led Ignatius to this diversity, the character of coadjutors, the learning necessary for the professed, the number of these and of spiritual coadjutors. Granero thinks that the professed must always be priests, bound to the pope with a very special tie (p. 50). "The 'select learning' required in their case is precisely that of the ecclesiastical sciences. . . .

They alone form the Society properly as such" (p. 50).

99. Lazslo Lukács, S.J. "De graduum diversitate inter sacerdotes in Societate Jesu." *AHSJ*, 37 (1968), 238-317.

St. Ignatius, foreseeing that not many men already learned would enter the Society, instituted the grade of spiritual coadjutors, that is, Jesuit priests who could devote themselves entirely to those ministries for which much learning was not necessary. Spiritual coadjutors, like many priests of that era, did not have more in the way of ecclesiastical studies than "cases of conscience." Their doctrinal formation was gradually increased. It seemed that in proportion to the better formation which the spiritual coadjutors received, their number would decrease. But the opposite occurred, owing, it would seem, to the opinion of Nadal, which is different from that of Ignatius. Nadal thought that to become professed one had to have "conspicuous" learning, and not merely "sufficient" learning. This opinion prevailed in such wise that the proportion of professed was greatly reduced by 1600. Only after that date did their number grow, and in such a manner that by 1773 the professed were 94.9% of the Society's priests and the spiritual coadjutors 5.1%.

An English digest of this study is in *The Constitutions of the Society of Jesus: Translated* . . . by G. E. Ganss, S.J. (no. 11 above), pp. 349-356. See also ibid., pp. 71, 81, 232.

100. Louis Renard, S.J. "La clase de indiferentes segun las Constituciones de la Compañía." Pp. 199-206 in *Congreso Internacional de Hermanos* (no. 67 above).

The author explains the meaning of the various redactions of the General Examen in those sections which refer to those who enter as indifferents. He does the same for the further dispositions of general congregations, actual practice in our history, and today's problematic.

101. There are also various mimeographed or lithographed monographs,
such as *Relatio Commissionis de Gradibus in Societate*
(Rome: Curia P. Generalis, 1969), and Gervais Dumeige, S.J.,
*De mente sancti Ignatii et posteriore evolutione historica
in quaestione de gradibus in Societate Iesu,* (Rome, 1969).

P. *The Novices*

102. Jesús M. Granero, S.J. "La Compañía de Jesús y sus novicios
(1540 a 1556)." *Manresa*, 42 (1970), 313-352.
  St. Ignatius came gradually to define the conditions
and characteristics which were to be verified in candidates
for the Society. He insisted on selectivity. He began by
summoning to Rome for purposes of a more adequate formation
those who offered greater promise. In the beginning, the
noviceship was carried on within the communities of priests,
but little by little the idea of establishing houses of
formation began to ripen. Granero indicates those which
were opened in the time of St. Ignatius, the evolution
which the various "trials" (*experiencias*) underwent, and
the kind of formation given to the novices. Likewise, he
indicates the development which took place in respect to
the vows of the scholastics. The practice was not the
same everywhere. Especially at the beginning, the vows
were private, but with the special connotation that the
Society was admitting them as "approved scholastics."

Q. *Prayer*

  Here we limit ourselves to Ignatian legislation on
the prayer of Jesuits. On prayer in general, see *Orientaciones bibliográficas sobre san Ignacio,* nos. 590-627.

103. Pedro de Leturia, S.J. "La hora matutina de meditación en la

Compañía naciente (1540-1590)." *AHSJ*, 3 (1934), 47-86
and, for ". . . documenta selecta," 87-108. These articles
were reprinted in Leturia's *Estudios Ignacianos*, edited by
Ignacio Iparraguirre, S.J., on pages 189-265 of vol. I,
Estudios biográficos. Vol. II contains the *Estudios espirituales*. Bibliotheca Instituti Historici S.I., nos.
10, 11. Rome: Institutum Historicum S.I., 1957. Pp. xxxii
+ 475 and viii + 544.

In these two volumes Father Leturia's works on St.
Ignatius are gathered together in their final form. His
acknowledged competence and mastery over his material is
reflected in these profound studies on the principle problem areas of the life and spirituality of St. Ignatius.

These two articles on prayer form a basic work which
supplants the earlier work of Pierre Bouvier, S.J., "Les
origines de l'oraison mentale dans la Compagnie de Jésus,"
Lettres de Jersey, 36 (Roehampton, 1923), 228-234. We
list this latter work here because of its novel way of
setting forth the lines of the problem and for some in-
teresting perspectives.

The gist of Leturia's studies on prayer can be found
in English in Joseph de Guibert, S.J., trans. W. J. Young,
S.J., *The Jesuits: Their Spiritual Doctrine and Practice*
(St. Louis: The Institute of Jesuit Sources, 1964 and 1972),
pages 86-90, 169, 192-196, 205, 222, 227-229, 237, 552-554.

104. On the legislation on prayer, see also studies produced on the
occasion of General Congregation XXXI: (1) Robert E.
McNally, S.J., in *Woodstock Letters*, 94 (1965), 108-134;
and especially, Miguel A. Fiorito, S.J., "Relatio I,
historica, circa legislationem Ignatianam et post-Igna-
tianam de oratione in Societate Iesu," in pages 46-90 of
Documenta selecta Congregationis Generalis XXXI (Rome:
Centrum Ignatianum Spiritualitatis, 1970). This *Relatio*
appeared in 1966, before Session II of General Congregation XXXI. After the Congregation Fiorito revised this

work and incorporated a commentary on decree 14: "La ley ignaciana de la oración en la Compañía de Jesús," *Stromata* (Buenos Aires), 23 (1967), 3–89. An English translation of the Spanish article, by Aloysius A. Jacobsmeyer, S.J., "Ignatius' Own Legislation on Prayer in the Society of Jesus," appeared in *Woodstock Letters*, 97 (1968), 149–224). This was reprinted by the Progam to Adapt the Spiritual Exercises, Jersey City, New Jersey, in 1970.

In the original Latin article of 1966, Fiorito presented a bibliography of previous works on the topic and a chronological list of 219 documents in primary sources, including all the passages on prayer in St. Ignatius' writings. Then he examined the role of the superior and of the subject in this area; he pointed out the manner of praying, the time which should be given to prayer and, by way of conclusion, offered a judgment on the variations in Ignatius' legislation on this point. The Ignatian prescriptions blossom out of the "deeper essence of the Spiritual Exercises, which consists in a dynamic balance between (1) the freedom, discretion, generosity, and responsibility of each subject and (2) the discretion, knowledge, and experience of the superior or spiritual director." In the Ignatian legislation there is a "marvelous and dynamic balance of liberty and law; and if this is disturbed by an excess of legislation, . . . a lack of responsibility and generosity of the subjects immediately appears" (pp. 89–90). The chief texts are *Cons* [340–342, 582–583].

R. *The Vows*

1. *Obedience in General*

We have thought it useful to indicate once more the principal works on Ignatian obedience in general, even those which do not refer directly to obedience as treated in the Constitutions. It is impossible to understand fully

the scope of St. Ignatius' prescriptions on obedience in
the Constitutions if account is not taken of the saint's
integral thought on this matter.

105. Miguel Angel Fiorito, S.J. "St. Ignatius' Intuitions on Obedience and Their Written Juridical Expression." *Woodstock
Letters*, 95 (1966), 137-142.

St. Ignatius sought in obedience the fulfillment of
a triple function: the union of the members with themselves
and with their head; apostolic cohesiveness; and a community of members who are separated by distance or for other
reasons. It is a bond which takes into account the entire
body. It is this communion that constitutes the soul of
obedience.

On the other hand, in its juridical expression, prom-
inence is given to the pre-eminence of the head over the
members, which "tends to emphasize the authority and its
sufficiency" (p. 139). In Ignatius' practice subjects
often participated much in the process which led to the
superior's decision. But historical evolution after Ignatius' death obscured this role of the subject. The
resolution of conflicts stemming from this one-sided or
excessive stress on the role of the suprior lies in seeking the living and spiritual source of the juridical expressions and considering the necessity of both a unifying
principle and a juridical structure for the cohesion of
the members among themselves and with their head.

106. Jesús Iturrioz, S.J. "Dos líneas de 'obediencia' en la Compañía de Jesús." *Manresa*, 43 (1971), 59-78.

There are two levels to be observed in the Society
in regard to obedience, the one of a more corporate nature,
and the other more directly pertaining to its mission and
apostolicity. The former corresponds to the internal requirements of the body of the Society. It is an interior
obedience which coordinates the members with their head

and among themselves. The latter directs the apostolic
activity of the Society. In Parts VII and IX of the Constitutions, which are focused on this second aspect, we
find in structured form our apostolic mission which takes
its point of departure from the supreme pontiff. In the
beginning, there was in fact greater dependence on the
pope, but soon the acts of obedience "came to focus on a
single person, the superior general of the Society, who
was the pope's delegate in regard to missions, whether
among the faithful or among the infidels" (p. 78). Per-
haps this confluence onto one and the same person has con-
tributed to a clouding of the precision and clarity of the
scope of each of these two types of obedience. But both
continue to retain their validity.

107. Marceliano Llamera, O.P. "La crisis actual de la obediencia
y las razones tradicionales e ignacianas de su necesidad."
Teología espiritual (Valencia), I (1957), 417-452.

After his analysis of the causes of the crisis of
obedience, Father Llamera examines the theological foundations of obedience, especially as based on St. Thomas and
on St. Ignatius, and then reviews the principal objections
against obedience.

108. Luis Mendizábal, S.J. *El modo perfecto de obedecer según san
Ignacio*. Colección Ruah, no. 2. Bérriz: Angeles de las
misiones, 1967. Pp. 48.

With respect to obedience in an order which is specifically Ignatian, a man submits himself in faith primarily
to God and his good pleasure, and secondarily to a man as
the visible mediator of that good pleasure. To explain
this manner of obeying, the author examines first the act
of obedience, and then the personal structure of him who
obeys. As regards the act of obedience, the Jesuit is
obliged to obey the superior in all things which touch
on the Institute of the Society. He ought to recognize

Christ as present in the superior, and this in a perfect
way, that is, by acknowledging, according to supernatural
light and under the action of grace, the objective order
of obedience as this is set forth by Ignatius with the
approval of the Church. This implies the obedience of
execution, will, and judgment, that is, a total and affective adhesion, with a corresponding affective rejection
of all other considerations. This is what will lead to a
conformity of the judgment--provided that this is not
rendered objectively impossible, as would happen were
there to be question of some sin.

The structure of obedience affects the whole person.
A new interior structure and dynamic of obedience progressively permeates the personality. The entire affective
and volitional complex, in the same way as the intellectual
part, should find itself dominated by obedience. This demands a basic disposition of humility and meekness, in
faith, love, and hope, so as to arrive at the holocaust
of oneself within the ambit of the Church. In this fashion, the whole person will remain integrated under obedience.

See also, by the same Luis Mendizabal, "El 'hecho
eclesiástico' de la obediencia ignaciana," *Manresa,* 36
(1964), 403-420; also "De oboedientia Societatis Jesu,"
pages 134-139 in *Documenta selecta Congregationis Generalis
XXXI* (no. 39 above).

109. Thomas H. O'Gorman, S.J. *Jesuit Obedience from Life to Law:
The Development of the Ignatian Idea of Obedience in the
Jesuit Constitutions, 1539-1556.* Manila: Loyola House of
Studies, Ateneo de Manila University, 1971. Pp. 116.

The process of Ignatian legislation on obedience,
realized through the saint's reflection on his various
experiences, is an example of Ignatius' openness to the
action of God. St. Ignatius proceeds by discerning, in
the light of the Spirit, various cases; and in the Con-

stitutions he crystalizes the results of this discernment.
From this fact arises the importance of his correspondence
for reaching an understanding of the scope of the various
phases of his legislation.

Obedience enshrines much of the soul and of the spirituality of the saint. "At one time the stress is rather
mystical, with obedience emphasized as the vehicle of union
with Christ, or even as the means by which spiritual bless-
ings are showered upon the members of the Society. At another time the accent is ascetical with attention directed
to abnegation of the will, exercise in humility, and the
like. The explanation for this difference in ascetical-
mystical stress lies partly in the different degrees of
membership. In one case obedience is presented to those
in probation and in the other to fully formed Jesuits"
(p. 99).

Union is a fundamental element in obedience. Through
it is realized union with God, with superiors, and with
the other members. This union is in function with the
apostolic finality of the Society.

110. Hugo Rahner, S.J. "De sensu theologico oboedientiae in Societate Iesu." Pp. 203-226 in *Documenta selecta Congregationis Generalis XXXI* (no. 45 above).

The author, having indicated the principal difficulties against Ignatian obedience, establishes the fundamental
principle: Perfect Ignatian obedience is the way of re-
sponding to the demands of the Exercises, especially, in
the concrete, to the end formulated in the First Principle
and Foundation. Obedience, in the proper sense, can be
given "to Christ the Lord, and only to him" (p. 211).
Ignatius demands obedience to the pope and to superiors
only to the extent that their wills are identified with
that of God. Because of this he insists on the presence
of God in the superiors, and looks for the greatest iden-
tification possible between Christ and superiors, espe-

cially the supreme pontiff. "All obedience in the Society
is the ultimate result of the vow of obedience to the supreme pontiff; but also, because of this reduction to the
vow to the pope and of his position in relation to Christ,
obedience in the Society constitutes service and praise
of God himself, our Creator and Lord (p. 12). The pope
is the vicar of "the crucified Lord of the Church." Therefore, to understand the theology of obedience fully, it is
necessary to take account of the theology of the cross,
which is also the basis for the theology of the Exercises.
The meaning of the holocaust of obedience finds here its
ultimate foundation. Obedience is a sharing in the redemptive work of Christ, and thus it is collaboration in establishing the Kingdom of Christ. The asceticism of obedience is founded in these theological realities. But
obedience is also based on the normal mode of collaboration
with God, who makes use of the faculties of man to accomplish His work. Hence the place of representation and of
co-responsibility in obedience.

111. Karl Rahner, S.J. "Eine ignatianische Grundhaltung: Marginalien
über den Gehorsam." *Stimmen der Zeit*, 158 (1956), 253-267;
2nd ed. in *Sendung und Gnade: Beiträge zur Pastoraltheologie*
(Innsbruck: Tyrolia-Verlag, 1959), pp. 493-516. An English
translation is in *Woodstock Letter*, 86 (1957), 291-310; also in *Christian in the Market Place* (New York, Sheed and
Ward, 1966) pp. 157-181. A full summary in Spanish was
made by Jesus Granero, S.J., in *Manresa*, 29 (1957), 69-72.

112. Manuel M. Espinosa-Pólit, S.J. *La obediencia perfecta: Commentario a la carta de la obediencia de san Ignacio de
Loyola.* Quito: Ed. Ecuatoriana, 1940. Pp. 446. 2nd ed.,
(Mexico: Ed. Jus., 1961). Pp. 396. Translated into English by William J. Young, S.J.: *Perfect Obedience*. West-
minster, Maryland: Newman Press, 1947. Pp. xiii + 331.
    This book is a commentary of great and basic impor-

tance. On it see C. de Dalmases, S.J., in *AHSJ*, 1 (1941), 168-169; and also *AHSJ*, 31 (1962), 400-401.

113. On the comparisons with the staff, the dead body and other such metaphors, see Pinard de la Boullaye, S.J., "La spiritualité ignatienne"(Paris: Plon, 1949), pp. 290-294.

114. François Roustang. "Analyse d'un texte de saint Ignace sur l'obéissance." *RAM*, 42 (1966), 31-37.

    The author analyzes *Constitutions*, [547], ch. 1 of Part VII. In it he finds three phases or steps which characterize the genesis of Ignatian obedience: (1) to dispose oneself; (2) to be effectively available (*disponible*); and (3) to allow oneself to be governed by God. These three phases are correlative to the essential moments of every election: to be indifferent or impartial, and to proceed by doing everything under a motion from God. "This leads us to identify the genesis of obedience with that of liberty and to consider obedience as another name of liberty" (p. 37).

2. *The Vow of Obedience to the Pope*

115. Burkhart Schneider, S.J. "Nuestro principio y principal fundamento. Zum historischen Verständnis des Papstgehorsamsgelübdes." *AHSJ*, (1956), 488-513.

    The author expounds that according to the mind of St. Ignatius, at least from 1539 on, the vow of obedience to the supreme pontiff was the fundamental vow, the total engagement, the *oblatio* or ideal to which the First Fathers then aspired. In their concept the general vow of obedience was something subsidiary. St. Ignatius did not follow through by having this concept reflected in the official documents.

116. Jesús M. Granero, S.J. "San Ignacio de Loyola al servicio de la Iglesia." *La ciencia tomista*, 83 (1956), 526-572.

Granero examines the internal evolution, gradual and often unconscious, through which St. Ignatius arrived at his special conception of this vow, which he believes to be even more important and central than the above listing would have. Father B. Schneider wrote a reply in *Gregorianum*, 39 (1958), 137-146.

117. Jesús M. Granero, S.J. *San Ignacio de Loyola: Panoramas de su vida*. Madrid: Razon y Fe, 1967. Pp. xxxi + 554.

In this work the author gathers together and updates his ideas on the vow of obedience to the pope, and also on most all of the other chief topics he has treated during his many years of publishing about St. Ignatius. A good index aids the reader to find quickly rich and scholarly treatment of most of the important aspects of St. Ignatius' life and work. There are also 14 pages of bibliography.

118. Johannes Günter Gerhartz, *"Insuper promitto." Die feierlichen Sondergelübde katholischer Orden*. Rome: Gregorian University Press, 1966. On pages 209-285 he relates this vow to the grouping of the "four vows" of other religious Institutes.

See also Luis M. Mendizabal, S.J. "Sensus oboedientiae specialis erga Pontificem apud Ignatium." *Periodica de re morali, canonica, liturgica*, 55 (1966), 601-604.

119. Antoine Delchard, S.J. "De quarto sollemni voto peculiaris oboedientiae Summo Pontifici circa missiones." Pp. 33-45 in *Documenta selecta Congregationis Generalis XXXI* (no. 45 above).

Father Delchard has studied the vow in its juridical implications. He first offers a synthesis of its historical development, rooting it especially in the vow of Montmartre, in the offering to the pope, and in the deliberations of 1539. By way of conclusion, he establishes a distinction between (1) the special fourth vow of obedience

to the pope which "will be defined according to the law
and practice of the Roman Curia, and its importance will
be seen undiminished in relation to the previous period"
and (2) the Society's peculiar obedience, which is related
to the vow above, which clearly seems to derive from it,
and which will preserve all its fundamental character and
value from it" (p. 37). He continues a juridical study of
the value of the fourth vow and of its relation to the general vow of obedience.

3. The Ignatian Style of Government

120. John C. Futrell, S.J., in *Making an Apostolic Community of Love*
(no. 79 above).

This book treats also of the role which St. Ignatius
assigns to the superior. The superior has an ecclesial
function. He should promote the vocation proper to the
Society. He is the servant of Christ for the sake of help-
ing his companions in their mission and in their ideals.
The highest superior is the Holy Father. The other superiors are the bridge between the pope and the rest of
the Jesuits. He should unite the members in a mutual love
so that they might fulfil their corporate apostolate in the
service of Christ.

In order that he might effectively bring this union
into being, "the superior after the process of mutual discernment makes the final decision and issues a command
which all the companions obey." Futrell sets forth as the
basis of his work the terms which St. Ignatius uses to indicate the various ways of exercising authority. Among these
terms which have an important place are discernment, representation, the communitarian climate of love, and the style
of exercising authority.

121. Jacques Lewis, S.J. *Le gouvernement spiritual selon saint Ignace de Loyola.* Studia: Recherches de philosophie et de

théologie publiées par les facultés S.J. de Montréal, no.
12. Montréal: Desclée de Brouwer, 1961. Pp. 139.

Lewis studies the spiritual government of St. Igna-
tius--and not just his constitutional or religious govern-
ment--in order to see how the action of the Holy Spirit
was joined in each soul with the action of the superior.
And this because the fundamental principle, according to
St. Ignatius, of the primordial function of the superior
is to make possible the full action of the Holy Spirit in
the community.

He examines Ignatius' practice in government and also
the spiritual principles and foundations on which this practice depends. The saint appears as extremely attentive to
the Holy Spirit. It is for this reason that he demands at
the same time a strict obedience and he leaves also a wide
margin for the personal initiative of the subjects; for he
was convinced that the subjects also "were personally en-
lightened by the Holy Spirit." The ultimate spiritual foundation is an organic vision of God's plan for the world and
for the position which each religious performs within this
total design. For reviews, see Gabriel de l'Annonciation,
O.C.D., *Sciences ecclésiastiques*, 15 (1962), 334-339; G.
Dumeige, S.J., *La civiltà cattolica*, 114 (1963), I, 157-
158.

122. Luis Mendizábal, S.J. *El modo de mandar según san Ignacio*.
Colección Ruah, no. 1. Bérriz: Angeles de las misiones,
1966. Pp. 40.

St. Ignatius' took a very great interest in making
sure that the order of obedience in the Society would be
well founded juridically. The foundation is found in the
Bull of Julius III and in the Constitutions, where the superior is endowed with power even in the field of conscience.
The superior should command that which he knows to be conducive to the end which God and the Society have established
for him with an objective and supernatural connection. Once

given, the order of the superior brings it about that
there arise such a connection at least reductively, in so
far as "it is to the greater glory of God and the good of
souls that the subject obey the valid order of the superior,
provided that this is not clearly sinful" (pp. 19-20). Then,
what the superior has commanded is conducive to the end.

It is necessary that the superior be chosen by reason
of his qualities. These can be seen in the *Constitutions*,
[423], and in the traits of a general, which are to be
proportionately applicable also to all superiors (ibid.,
[723-725]). The superior should command after he has sufficient information, after suitable prayer and with a mor-
tified judgment, leaning on the grace of state, with kind-
ness and meekness. Consequently, he should not measure
out for his subjects according to measurements proper to
himself. Many times he will leave to the subject the
ability to reform orders, accommodating them to circumstances, as the divine will manifests itself to spiritual
men who are truly prudent in Christ.

4. *Poverty*

123. "The Deliberation on Poverty of St. Ignatius." The text, written
in 1544, is in *Cons*MHSJ, I, 78-83. (no. 5 above); also in
Obras completas de san Ignacio, 2nd edition (no. 6 above),
pp. 293-299, with the transcription, introduction, and
notes done by Ignacio Iparraguirre, S.J.

An English translation of the Deliberation on Poverty
is found on pages 61-63 of *The Spiritual Journal of St.
Ignatius Loyola, February, 1544-45*, translated by W. J.
Young, S.J. Woodstock College Press, 1958; reprint at
Jersey City: Program to Adapt the Spiritual Exercises,
1971.

A part of this Deliberation has been translated into
French on pages 6-8 of *Notes ignatiennes, 1556-1956. In-
troductory texts and translations by the Fathers of the*

Assistancy of France. Enghien: La maison Saint-Augustin, 1956. Note 2, pp. 6-8.

124. Joseph Creusen, S.J. "La pauvreté de saint Ignace", *La pauvreté (Problèmes de la religieuse d'aujourd'hui)*. Paris: Ed. du Cerf, 1952. Pp. 85-98.

125. Antoine Delchard, S.J. "La génèse de la pauvreté ignatienne." *Christus*, 6 (1959), no. 24, 464-496.

Ignatius first practiced the poverty of a solitary mendicant, later, that of a small fraternity: "Following the example of St. Francis of Assisi, he aims with some companions to lead an evangelical life in which poverty is simultaneously a form of life and the essential content of the preaching" (p. 465). In the third stage, drawing near now to the early experiences of the Dominicans, he adopts the traditional forms of mendicant poverty in religious life (ibid.).

There is a two-fold line in the entire constitutional structuration. On one side, there is fidelity to the tradition of the mendicant orders--in the concrete, that of the Dominicans with their mendicant communities for apostolic works; and on the other side, for the scholastics in their studies he returns to the monastic tradition, wherein he foresees at once the possession of a common patrimony and personal poverty.

126. Miguel Angel Fiorito and Guilermo Hueyo, S.J. "Pobreza personal y pobreza institucional." *Stromata*, 21 (1965), 325-355.

In the first part the authors treat of "The Ignatian concept of personal poverty." Ignatius, following spiritual tradition in this matter, regards poverty as a total attitude and not a particular form of life, as a gesture of the whole man, not only in regard to his house or his temporal goods, but with respect to everything that is

not God. Wealth is not an evil in itself, but only in
so far as it draws away from confidence in God and detains
man among temporal goods. The basic solution is not a
poverty of want, but a freedom of spirit, or a liberating
poverty before everything that is not God nor one's neighbor.

In the second part, Fiorito examines institutional
poverty. The Ignatian legislation reflects those sources
of support which were operative in the socio-economic order
in which the saint moved: fixed or regularly recurring rev-
enue (*renta*), manual labor, and alms. At that time the
three sources were viewed in a good light. There were no
manifest abuses in regard to fixed revenues, nor were alms
regarded as a sign of oppression. On the other hand, manual labor was considered as a hindrance from the point of
view of spiritual and apostolic concern. St. Ignatius
made use of all three sources: the colleges possessed in-
come from fixed revenues, the apostolic workers lived off
alms, and the coadjutors from their labor; but Ignatius
integrated this use of temporal goods into a more ample
conception of an apostolic order. Obedience regulates
the practice of poverty. The vow does not inhibit a certain use of things which does not cause a loss of freedom
of spirit, and which helps to the improvement and redemption of man.

For all these reasons, one ought to distinguish between the concrete determinations of St. Ignatius as to
how poverty was to be lived in his time, and poverty itself. "To live on alms used to be the symbol par excel-
lence of confidence in God. But this symbol has become
obscure today. Its place has been taken by the terrible
reality that the one who lives on alms declares himself
to be impotent before his own situation and that of others;
and also that he lives in dependence on those who have
caused this situation" (p. 346). Today demands not only
that one live in poverty, but that he preach poverty and

defend the poor. St. Ignatius chose a form in which poverty of obedience prevailed over poverty of want. True
poverty implies a charity placed at the service of man in
his progress toward well-being both here and hereafter.

127.   Jesús M. Granero, S.J. "La pobreza ignaciana." *Manresa*, 40
       (1968), 149-174.

       At the beginning of his life of conversion, the saint
ambitioned the following of an absolute poverty conformed
to the examples he had found in the *Flos sanctorum*. Poverty was for him that of a mendicant: to receive in alms
what was necessary for life, without having any economic
reserve. In the time of his studies, this poverty took
on various forms, but the ideal was always the same. In
Rome in the first years, he lived with his companions in
austere houses and without any comforts. He supported
himself by alms and spontaneous donations. But he took
no note of costs when there was question of health, and
saw to it that there was sufficient food to permit work.
He did not permit remuneration for ministries, because
for him apostolic labor was not productive. There re-
mained to him no other source of support than the charity
of the neighbor. This was his practice. In the case of
the colleges, he assured support through the obligatory
granting of some capital and of some fixed revenues. The
other houses proceeded by meeting current necessities on
the basis of alms and donations.

       The work with the poor can also be a witness. St.
Ignatius, although he worked much with the poor, did not
establish as an explicit criterion for the choice of ministries the poverty or wealth of the persons served, but
the urgency or necessity of the work. He had a ministry
which was almost always carried on among children or the
poor, the teaching of catechism. He also paid charitable
heed to many underprivileged, hungry and homeless in periods of famine.

128. Miguel Mendizábal, S.J. "La pobreza, virtud apostólica según san Ignacio." *Manresa*, 42 (1970), 203-222.

The author presents the norms of Ignatius on the poverty which is suited for apostolic workers. "All these, in their demands and scrupulous concerns, tend toward placing the necessity for total disinterestedness in high relief. . . . The [apostolic workers] ought to proceed in such manner that no one could even suspect that the motive of their action has been influenced by the desire for gain or for material profit" (p. 206).

The profound reason for these directives rests upon the fact that in this manner the worker embraces Christ poor. There were some who interpreted this living on alms as arrogance or presumption. But generally this mode of procedure was a source of edification and apostolic efficiency by reason of the freedom of spirit it produced. Benefactions were recognized as coming from God more than from benefactors, and in this way the freedom for the ministries was not diminished.

129. Günter Switek, S.J., *In Armut predigen. Untersuchungen zum Armutsgedanken bei Ignatius von Loyola.* München: Echter Verlag, 1972. Pp. 308.

Switek examines the evolution and experimental efforts of Ignatius as he felt his way toward combining the most rigid personal poverty with the problems of an apostolic order. He analyzes the various influences, including those which the saint experienced before his conversion, delaying especially on the influence exercised by the legislation of older religious orders.

With the problem set against this background, he analyzes the characteristics of poverty according to the Constitutions and the practice of Ignatius. Economic difficulties, the rapid growth of the order, and apostolic necessity forced a compromise on the practice. But Ignatius, having passed through the inevitable fluctuations

of such experiences, soon returned to the primitive form
of poverty.

Poverty for the saint was an essential attitude of
Christ, and so no one could possibly imitate Christ without being truly poor. Further, the apostolic life demanded
the witness of poverty which, of itself, has a strong apostolic force. After much reflection and experimentation,
he decided to admit, not two forms of poverty in one house,
but two forms of poverty in diverse types of dwellings,
the houses and the colleges.

130. Hugo Rahner, S.J. "Historica quaedam de paupertate in Societate
Iesu." *Documenta selecta Congregationis Generalis XXXI*
(no. 45 above), pp. 155-170.

The author describes the poverty of Ignatius first
of all throughout the course of his life, since the procedures of poverty in the Society follow those of its
founder. Then he examines the successive phases of legislation.

131. Hugo Rahner, S.J. "Historica quaedam de voto non-relaxandae
paupertatis." Ibid., pp. 172-181.

The author studies the occasion and the object of the
vow. According to him, the vow is not extended, as Suárez
affirms, to the whole matter of poverty, but pertains sole-
ly to the specific object of the vow: the transferring of
the poverty proper to the one type of Jesuit dwellings to
the type of the others (p. 181).

132. Hugo Rahner, S.J. "Historica quaedam de gratuitate ministe-
riorum." Ibid., pp. 182-202.

To understand the problem, Rahner first examines the
historic evolution of stipends for Mass, focusing principally on the abuses to which this practice had given place.
From this historical survey, Rahner deduces the conclusion
that when Ignatius "used the word *stipendium*, he was think-

ing of a 'stipendium formatum,' that is, one given precisely
'as recompense' for a spiritual ministry. Therefore he was
seeking to avoid a juridical connection between a spiritual
work and temporal thing" (p. 191). He thinks also (ibid.)
that "Gratuity in the Constitutions cannot be understood
except in the light of the Counter-Reformation, especially
in what pertains to the gratuity of Masses. . . . We are
today more certain . . . that the law of gratuity does not
belong to the substance of the vow of poverty, although it
is intimately linked with the purity of poverty" (*Constitutions*, [816]). . . . "Insofar as our gratuity of ministries is apostolic, it ought to be evaluated as a means
or instrument (and not as some sort of absolute which
stands by itself), in accordance with the end, liberty
of action and the edification of the neighbor, as *Constitutions*, [565] states" (p. 192).

Rahner concludes (p. 202) by citing St. Thomas: "Perfection does not consist essentially in poverty, but in the
following of Christ. Therefore each religious institute
will be more perfect in regard to poverty in proportion to
its having a poverty adjusted to its end" (*Summa theologiae*,
II-II, Q. 188, a. 7). Suárez applied this same doctrine to
the poverty of the Society.

133. David B. Knight, S.J. "Saint Ignatius' Ideal of Poverty."
Studies in the Spirituality of Jesuits, 4 (1972), 1-37.
St. Louis: The American Assistancy Seminar on Jesuit Spir-
ituality, 1972.

The poverty characteristic of the Jesuit is not only
spiritual, but also real in the sense that his should be
a life which serves for edification to all and which re-
sponds to the ideal of abnegation, a work which is properly apostolic. His life should be readily recognized as
poor to the man of today, having no extraordinary posses-
sions, and at times even deprived of necessities. He
should experience something of material insecurity, pre-

supposing that his life is founded on divine hope and on
supernatural resources. His life is lived in the joy of
reproducing in it the ideal of service and of humility
that was given by Christ our Lord.

134. Also worthy of consultation on this topic are: Josef Wicki, S.J.
"Pfarrseelsorge und Armut der Professhaüser: . . . Ein Motu
proprio Pauls III aus der vorgeschichte des römischen Gesu
(1549)." *AHSJ*, 11 (1942), 69-82.

Antonio M. de Aldama, S.J. The first part of "La
forma de los contratos de alienación en la Compañía de
Jesús desde san Ignacio al P. Acquaviva," *AHSJ*, 25 (1956),
539-573.

The studies on Ignatius' *Spiritual Diary* which are
listed in *OrientBibliograf*, nos. 475-581.

The numbers refer to the marginal references, e.g. 8.

Abad, Camil, S.J., ed., 21, 22

Account of Conscience, 84, 85

Aicardo, José Manuel, S.J., 28

Aldama, Antonio de, S.J.,
  on coadjutors, 97
  on composition of Constitu-
    tions, 10, 16
  on reading Cons, 39
  form of Contracts, 134

Alvarez, Baltasar, S.J., 21

Anel, Emilio, S.J., 1

Apostolic activity, 67, 68

Archivum Historicum S.J., 2

Arndt, Aug., S.J., ed., 25

B

Barjavisi, Alejo, rev., 22

Baruffo, Antonio, S.J., 87

Baumann, Theodor, S.J., 58, 59

Bednarz, M., S.J., tr., 12

Benitez, José E., S.J., 69

Besson, Julius, ed., 35

Boado, Faustino, S.J., ed., 21

Boero, José, ed., 23

Bojorge, Horacio, S.J., tr., 91

Bouvier, Pierre, S.J., 103

Broughton, William G., 11

Brouwer, Theodorus, tr., 36

C

Canisius, St. Peter, *Exhortations*, 19

Carli, Laurent, S.J., tr., 24

Chastonay, Paul de, S.J., 17, 29

Coadjutors:
  spiritual, 97, 99, 100
  temporal, 69-76
  See also Grades

Codina, Arturo, S.J.,
  ed., 5, 16, 17
  Examen and Cons, 51

Codina , Victor, S.J., rev., 10

Coemans, Auguste, S.J., 30
  See also 33

Colleges, 77, 78

Communal Deliberation, 86-92

Community, 79

*Congreso Internacional de Her-
  manos*, 67, 70, 71, 73, 74,
  100

Costa, Maurizio, S.J.,
  on Cons, 41
  interpretation of Cons, 55
  communitarian deliberation,
    88
  the Cons and hope, 95

Courel, François, S.J.,
  on Cons, 9, 62, 65;
  rev., 42, 79

Creusen, Joseph, S.J., 124

D